MW01289964

SHREWD AS SERPENTS
and
Innocent as Doves

A Practical Security Guide for Christian Travelers
SCOTT STEWART

Printed in the United States of America

ISBN-10: 1491063475
ISBN-13: 9781491063477

Publisher: Scott Stewart
Cover Design: Ben Sledge
Layout: TJ Lensing

CONTENTS

AUTHOR'S ACKNOWLEDGEMENTS

First, I want to acknowledge that if it were not for the way God has wired me as a person, and the various career and ministry doors He has opened to me during my lifetime, I would certainly not have the background and ability to write this book. As Psalm 103 says: "Let all that I am praise the Lord; may I never forget the good things He does for me."

Second, I'd like to thank my wife Jackie for encouraging me to finish this book and publish it despite the lack of interest in the project from the many literary agents and publishing companies I contacted. I would have given up on the project if not for her gentle persistence that such a book was sorely needed to keep missionaries and other Christian travelers safe. Jackie has stuck by me through my crazy career, and has also been my partner in ministry, to include leading several short-term mission trips. I love her with all my heart.

I would also like to thank my friends Dr. Scott Kennedy, Jim McDonald of Meeting God In Missions and David Pryor of New Tribes Missions who took time to read and critique final drafts of this book, as well as Carol Green, Fred Burton,

Mike Parks, Anya Alfano and Mike McCullar for their input on the initial draft of the first four chapters. Your time and efforts helped make this book better and your positive reactions to the material were a great encouragement to me!

I'd also like to thank Robin Blackburn for her editing magic, Ben Sledge for the cover graphics, and TJ Lensing for his help in formatting the book.

Finally, to the people reading this book who are traveling to carry out the Great Commission: MAY GOD BLESS YOU AND KEEP YOU SAFE AS YOU LABOR FOR HIS GLORY.

INTRODUCTION: PERILS

In hard traveling year in and year out, I've had to ford rivers, fend off robbers, struggle with friends, struggle with foes. I've been at risk in the city, at risk in the country, endangered by desert sun and sea storm, and betrayed by those I thought were my brothers.

— 2 Corinthians 11:16

I don't know if you've noticed, but the world has become a smaller place. In this era of low-cost airfares, ecotourism and adventure vacations, more and more people are exploring the wild and remote corners of the world. In addition to leisure travelers, a growing number of Americans are trekking to out-of-the-way parts of the world to participate in short-term mission trips. A generation ago, only a few intrepid souls dared to venture to mission fields that were very far off the beaten path, but that has changed. In fact, not too many years ago, it took missionaries weeks or even months just to get to their destinations — longer than the length of many short-term mission trips today. Additionally, many countries traditionally difficult for Westerners to travel to have liberalized their immigration policies, and countries that were previously considered "closed" are now open for tourism and missionary work. As a result, more people are traveling to more parts of the world than ever before.

Although the world may seem smaller today, it remains as dangerous as it ever was. As Christians, we know that ever since the fall of man, the earth has been filled with sin, greed and crime. That has not changed. However, the nature of the dangers Christian travelers face is somewhat different. The fears of cannibalistic tribesmen and tropical diseases have lessened, but the threats of terrorism and sophisticated and heavily armed criminals have replaced them. While some of the dangers in the world exist near our own homes, these dangers are magnified while we are traveling — when we are strangers in a strange land, coping with a sense of otherness and not belonging, and visibly sticking out in a crowd. Furthermore, criminals tend to target traveling Americans because of a general belief that their pockets are filled with cash, or that they otherwise have access to large sums of money. This assumption is generally true, because travel is costly and many Americans traveling abroad find it necessary to carry a large amount of cash (especially in locations that still do not widely accept credit cards or have many ATMs.) Additionally, even those of us who might not think of ourselves as rich are terribly wealthy when compared to most of the people we will encounter in the developing world, and this wealth makes us a target for criminals.

Unfortunately, thousands of Americans fall victim to criminals while they are traveling every year. What is even more unfortunate to my mind is that many of the people who are victimized didn't have to be. With a little education and preparation they could have taken steps that would have prevented an encounter with the criminal element or at least mitigated the effects of an encounter. I am writing this book to provide that education and preparation. I want to help people look for, recognize and avoid criminals who would seek to harm them.

Because of my background as a security expert, and my extensive experience as an overseas traveler, I am frequently asked for security advice and have provided travel security briefings to missionary organizations, church groups, friends, family members, student groups and short-term mission teams. I also lead a short-term mission group from my church every year, so I understand some of the ministry aspects as well.

The travel security briefings I have developed over the years are really an extension of what I did when I worked as a security officer at the U.S. Embassy in Guatemala City — a diplomatic post facing what was considered a critical crime threat. One of my duties there was to provide crime awareness and avoidance briefings to U.S. government employees living in or visiting Guatemala, as well as their spouses, children and household staff members.

I was also blessed with the opportunity to give personal and residential security briefings to groups of missionaries and other U.S. citizens residing in Guatemala through a series of lectures I gave at the church we attended there, the Union Church of Guatemala. In this way I was able to develop a very active ministry, teaching people about personal security and helping them avoid being victimized by criminals. This ministry allowed me to combine my skills and experience as a security expert with my passionate desire to help people stay safe.

The biggest difference between the briefings I do now and the briefings I did then is that I am no longer a U.S. government employee and can give my briefings with a decidedly Christian perspective. The practical principles I will lay out in this book can be used by any traveler, but readers who are easily offended by Christian principles would be best to avoid reading further.

One of the most significant things I want to share with you is the understanding that the situational awareness and threat recognition needed to avoid criminals are not super-secret skills that only highly trained experts can master. To the contrary, they are simple, common-sense principles that can be learned and practiced by anyone who has the will and discipline to employ them.

As much as I would like to, I simply don't have the ability to travel to every home and church in the United States to provide the content of my security briefing to everyone who is preparing to travel abroad. But my fervent hope and prayer is that by putting the content of my presentation into book form, I will be able to share the information with a far wider audience than I ever could in person.

CHAPTER ONE:
A CHRISTIAN PERSPECTIVE
ON PERSONAL SECURITY

The wise are cautious and avoid danger; fools plunge ahead with reckless confidence.

— Proverbs 14:16

International travel presents certain risks for Americans, especially in areas of the developing world where governments have less control, and law and order is not as formally established as it is in the United States. When you inject widespread poverty, the potential for cultural misunderstandings and a ready abundance of weapons into the mix, it can make for a volatile environment — an environment that causes us to assume greater responsibility for our own safety and practice a higher degree of situational awareness than we generally do at home, where we are able to rely more heavily on the authorities. Unfortunately, any incident that occurs in such an environment is generally more difficult to handle than a similar situation in the United States, and it can sometimes become very bad very quickly. Because of this, to steal an old wives' tale, an ounce of prevention is worth a pound of cure.

Most mission trips are, by definition, journeys into areas that have great needs — for food, clothing, shelter, clean water, medical attention and, most important, the gospel of Jesus Christ. But missionaries are not the only travelers who may find themselves in "interesting" places. Travelers wishing to visit Mayan ruins in Guatemala, photograph wildlife in Africa or tour Biblical sites in Turkey or Israel can also find themselves in a security environment that is quite different from what they are used to — an environment that can sometimes seem exciting, scary, or both.

One thing I would like to make abundantly clear is that this book is not intended to create paranoia or fear. Let me repeat that: I do not want to make you afraid to travel. Rather, I want to help you become informed, aware and prepared. This book has been written to educate you about how criminals operate and to help you learn how to practice situational awareness. Situational awareness — being aware of your environment and the people around you — is significantly different from paranoia, and the two should never be confused. Paranoia is an unfounded, exaggerated, irrational fear. As we will discuss in Chapter Three, the chapter that deals with situational awareness, paranoia and worry can not only have a disastrous effect on your mind and body but can also be counterproductive to your security. Therefore, the intent of this book is not to *scare* you, but to *prepare* you — prepare you for a safe and enjoyable journey. You can't enjoy your trip if you are looking for a criminal lurking behind every bush, and you can't minister to people if you fear them. But, conversely, it can be very difficult to enjoy your trip if you are injured in a robbery attempt, or if your luggage, medical equipment or tracts have been stolen. And all of these things can and do happen to Christian travelers. So what we are looking for is balance — an awareness that there are threats out there, but a relaxed awareness that also allows you to enjoy your trip and minister to others.

As to the threat, as Christians, we must recognize that the world is rife with sin, crime and violence. That is a Biblical fact, and the level of an observer's awareness — or ignorance — of this fact will not change the fallen condition of the world. It is what it is. The Bible itself tells us to expect trouble in this fallen world. Recognizing this condition and maintaining a rational awareness of the dangers around us allows us to be vigilant and prepared. These two things — vigilance and preparedness — will permit us to see potential problems as they develop and allow us time to take action to either avoid the problem or minimize the impact of the problem. If we are not vigilant and prepared, problems surprise us and we cannot avoid them.

It is also important for us to understand that there is risk in everything we do. There are even risks associated with driving to church or stepping into the bathtub. Travel is no exception; there are risks involved every time we take a trip. These risks are even greater if we are going into an area where there is dire need, widespread crime and little authority. However, we must also be mindful that amid the risks there are also tremendous rewards to be reaped, and there are times when we must step out in faith and take risks to share the gospel with people, or to otherwise help meet their needs. Simply put, some risks are worth taking. Remember, when Jesus told his disciples that they would face troubles in the world, He also told them to take heart because He had overcome the world.

That said, I do not believe it is wise — or Biblical, for that matter — to take such risks without first attempting to quantify them and fully understand what is being undertaken and the potential cost of that undertaking. When Jesus discussed the cost of being a disciple to his followers in Luke Chapter 14, He said to them: "Suppose one of you wants to build a tower. Will he not first sit down and estimate the cost to see if he has enough money to complete it? For if he lays the foundation and is not able to finish it, everyone who sees it will ridicule him, saying, 'This fellow began to build and was not able to finish.'" Clearly, Jesus wants us as His followers to do what we've been called to do, but He also wants us to have a clear understanding of what it is we have been called to and to be aware of the cost of our obedience.

Later on in that same passage, Jesus says that a disciple must be willing to abandon everything to follow Him. This means that if we believe we are being led by the Holy Spirit to do something, we must undertake that duty in spite of the risks that must be faced. However, I also believe it is clearly Biblical that we are not to be needlessly reckless with our lives and that we should undertake prudent measures to attempt to avoid or mitigate risk where possible — and where the means of avoiding risk are not at odds with our duty or the Word of God.

Some may think that being concerned about the risks associated with a ministry, or attempting to avoid or mitigate those risks, displays a lack of faith in God's love and protection. This is simply not true. Don't misunderstand me: Worry *is* wrong, and we are clearly told in Scripture not to worry, but it also important to understand that a prudent concern, and even a healthy respect, for the challenges facing us is not the same thing as worry. Worry is a prolonged process of repeatedly dwelling on the risk or threat. Weighing risks without constantly focusing on them, and then taking prudent steps to avoid or mitigate those risks, is very different from worrying, and this approach is, at least in my opinion, clearly more consistent with Biblical example than being ignorant of the risks — or worrying about them. But, in addition to ignorance and worry, there is a third course of behavior that I believe is un-Biblical, and that is recklessness.

In Matthew, Chapter Four, Jesus was being tempted by the Devil in the wilderness. After Jesus refused the Devil's suggestion to turn stones to bread to satisfy His hunger, the Devil took Jesus to Jerusalem and stood with Him on the highest point of the Temple there. "If you are the Son of God," the Devil said, "throw yourself down. For it is written: 'He will command his angels concerning you, and they will lift you up in their hands, so that you will not strike your foot against a stone.' But Jesus answered him, "It is also written: 'Do not put the Lord your God to the test.'"

In this passage, we can see by the example of Jesus Himself that believers are not to recklessly plunge themselves into danger. So, while we must step out in faith, and face challenges — and even danger — when we are called to, we should never do so in a reckless manner, as if to test God. Truly, God *is* in control, and He will care for us, but, that does not mean that we should needlessly put Him to the test by neglecting things we can do to care for ourselves. I believe it is disrespectful for us to put God needlessly to the test by running headlong into troubles we should have been able to avoid without reliance upon divine intervention. God has given us common sense, perception and people who can provide sound advice for a reason. We should not ignore them.

Speaking of advice, I also believe that it is clearly Biblical to listen to the counsel of wise men. This includes listening to security advice, which Paul modeled in the book of Acts on numerous occasions. For example, when Paul's companions were seized in Ephesus, he wanted to go into the theater where they were being held and attempt to rescue them. However, his friends and followers pleaded with him not to enter — and he heeded their advice. Paul was also warned in Tyre and in Caesarea about the dangers he would face on his final trip to Jerusalem, but he undertook the trip in spite of the warning because, although he knew the risk, he knew the trip was God's plan for him and he must proceed. It is also notable that once Paul was in Jerusalem and had done what he felt God called him to do, he did allow the Roman military to evacuate him from a very dire security situation. This was not unlike people today who occasionally have to be evacuated from dangerous situations by their governments. In other words, Paul's example shows us that listening to security advice and even allowing the government to provide us with assistance in an emergency does not mean that we are in any way less trusting of God's providence. Indeed, such things can be His providence to us.

We should also avoid placing ourselves at risk for the wrong reason. It is one thing to take a risk to minister to people and help spread the Gospel, or to go somewhere because we feel God's call to do so. It is another to take a risk merely for excitement or to be with our friends. We must ensure that any risk we endure is done with an eternal and not a worldly mindset.

There is also the Biblical principle of stewardship. The ministries we work in do not belong to us. They are God's ministries, and God has entrusted His ministries to us to manage for Him here on earth. We must recognize this and be wise stewards over the ministries and people entrusted to our care — and of our very lives, for that matter. We are not to endanger the things entrusted to us needlessly or negligently, and doubly so for the people we have been called to shepherd. Many Christians have no problem using alarm systems to protect their homes, churches or cars, yet somehow they seem to frown upon taking security measures to protect themselves, believing it demonstrates a lack of faith in God's providence and protection. But this concept is simply not true. There is nothing wrong or "un-Christian" about having a rational concern for our personal safety or about taking practical steps and using common sense to stay safe.

The Gospel of John refers to Jesus as the "Logos," which not only translates literally as "word" but also holds the deeper connotation of the fundamental order through which all things were made. "Logos" is also the Greek word from which the English word "logic" is derived. That means that Christ is the embodiment of logic, prudence, judgment and common sense. It should also be noted that, during His ministry, Jesus often combined the practical with the spiritual. An example of this was when He used saliva and dirt to form mud to heal the blind man. There was no "magic" in the mud, and Jesus, being the author of the universe, clearly had no need to use the mud — or anything else — to heal the man. He could have just willed the healing and it would have occurred instantly. However, in His wisdom He chose to use the ordinary to accomplish the divine and miraculous. This is why we must not look down on ordinary and practical things or fail to understand how God can use those things in His ministry to us — and to keep us safe. In my security briefings, I use the "Parable of the Pastor and the Flood" to illustrate this point.

Once, during a heavy flood, a small town located on the banks of a swollen river was being threatened by the rising waters. The pastor of the town's church was working with his congregation to save their church from the rapidly rising river. To do this, they feverishly filled and stacked sandbags in an attempt to keep the flood waters at bay. When the waters kept rising and did not show any sign of abating, the members of the congregation grew concerned about their own safety and told the pastor that they believed they should all evacuate to higher ground. The pastor told the congregation that they could evacuate, but that he was confident the Lord would never forsake him and he would stay put. The water continued to rise and just as it began to top the Church's sandbag levee, a National Guard truck came by the church and the guardsmen begged the pastor to leave with them. However, the pastor refused to leave and told the guardsmen that he was certain that God would never forsake him.

All that day, the water kept rising and the pastor was forced to climb into the choir loft of the church. A sheriff's deputy in a boat came by, noticed the pastor looking out of the choir loft window and offered to take the pastor to safety. Again, he refused. As the water continued to rise, the pastor was forced onto the roof of the church, and he was eventually forced to cling to the steeple of the church to keep the water from sweeping him away. A Coast Guard helicopter spotted him and sent down a harness to haul him to safety, but the pastor again refused to be helped. He was firmly convinced that the Lord would never leave him or forsake him. The water continued to rise, and it eventually swept the pastor from the steeple and he drowned.

When the pastor woke up, he found himself in Heaven, standing before the throne of Jesus. After he overcame the shock and beauty of being in Christ's presence, he looked into the face of Jesus and cried, "Lord, why did you forsake me?" Jesus looked at him lovingly and replied, "My son, I attempted to save you by using the members of your congregation and when that didn't work, I sent a truck, a boat and a helicopter to save you. You refused to let me save you."

While this is just a story, it does illustrate how God can help us through the mundane if we will allow Him.

Another Biblical model of personal security was David. He knew exactly what he was facing when he went out to meet Goliath. He also knew that he had been called to face the giant, and that he had to obey God's calling. God also required David to take some practical action in his own defense — David was forced to slay Goliath by himself. God did not do it for him. When faced with another threat, that of Saul, David listened to Jonathan's advice and fled to save his life. He did not recklessly stay put and wait for God to do everything for him. However, from the Psalms, we can see that, even in that circumstance, when he was running for his life, David believed that God was his strength, his shield and his protection.

Now, shifting our focus from the mundane to the supernatural, we must realize that there is also a spiritual aspect to all of the security threats that we face as Christians. We are not only facing the threat of evil and sinful men, but also the spiritual threat posed by Satan and his malicious host. Therefore, like everything else we do, our travel must be undergirded with prayer and led by the Holy Spirit. We should pray for safety and listen for the prompting of the Holy Spirit regarding security issues. I have personally interviewed several crime victims who disregarded feelings that warned them of danger and were then victimized. In a secular security briefing, I normally advise people to "follow your instincts." But now that I am speaking to a Christian audience, I can say so much more. I believe that, in addition to the instincts and subconscious God has designed within us, we have something more powerful that can warn us from danger — the Holy Spirit. He can guide us away from danger in much the same way He can steer us into ministry opportunities if we allow Him.

Therefore, we must listen to "the still, small voice" in addition to our instincts and subconscious. If something feels wrong or dangerous to you, it probably is. If something is telling you not to go down an alley, don't go. Of course, the converse is also true. If the Holy Spirit is leading us to an area that looks dangerous, we must obey.

Most missionaries travel to troubled places with altruistic motives and the genuine desire to help others. However, it is important to understand that your motives and your mission will not protect you, no matter how noble they are. In the eyes of criminals and terrorists, your motives for being in such a place and what you are attempting to accomplish are far less important than your monetary, symbolic or negotiating value. The fact that you are an American, a Christian or both — and that you are accessible — is far more significant to many malefactors than any good works you may be attempting to accomplish. Of course, this does not apply just to missionaries; secular NGO workers and journalists often run into the same problem. Therefore, you should never assume that your purpose for being in a place offers you any protection from harm.

Furthermore, Americans in particular have a tendency to consider themselves "citizens of the world" and sometimes think the rules of law and civilization allow them to go head-to-head in opposition to corrupt and violent foreigners in a position of local power, a formula for disaster as often as not. In many parts of the globe, there is no rule of law or of civilization, just the rule of force. Because of this, it is critical to do the homework necessary to understand where the power lies in a specific area, and how it might be expressed, before getting involved in local disputes.

Jesus gave us the bottom line regarding personal security in Matthew Chapter 10. When he was sending out the disciples,

He told them, "Behold, I send you out as sheep in the midst of wolves; so be shrewd as serpents and innocent as doves."

Being "shrewd as serpents" means that we are to be aware of the wolves and watch for them. Jesus tells his disciples to "be on your guard" in Verse 17. It also means that we should attempt to avoid their evil schemes wherever possible. Jesus tells his disciples, "When you are persecuted in one place, flee to another." Jesus also repeats several times in this passage that the disciples were not to fear. So while we need to recognize danger and avoid it, we must not worry or panic.

In this book, I will teach you how to watch for the wolves, how to recognize them and how to avoid some of their schemes without worry or fear. Now, before we go on, let's pause for a minute to pray together.

Dear Father God, I thank you that, in Your holiness, power and might, You, the awesome Creator of the universe, choose to care about us and for us. Lord, I pray that you will keep my brothers and sisters safe as they explore the wonder of Your creation and minister to the poor, the needy and the hopeless. Lord, allow them to be aware of the risks that exist in the environments they find themselves in, and I pray, Lord, that You will allow them to see and avoid the snares of wicked men and of the evil one. Father, guide their steps, draw them close to You and keep them safe in Your ever-loving arms. Amen.

CHAPTER TWO:
BEFORE YOU GO — RESEARCH
THE ENVIRONMENT

Let the wise listen and add to their learning, and let the discerning get guidance.

— Proverbs 1:5

Perhaps the best chance of remaining out of harm's way while traveling or working abroad is to know and understand — in advance — some of the idiosyncrasies of each country's bureaucracy and the security risks that have been identified for your intended location. Armed with this knowledge and guidance, you can plan and implement proper precautions. Fortunately, in the Internet age, finding safety and security information for your destination country is easier than ever.

Once a short-term mission team or full-time missionary has settled on a destination, it is wise to establish contact with the host organization to arrange all the details for the trip. In addition to addressing the normal logistical issues, you should also ask for information about the environment in which you will be ministering. This information should include local culture, laws, government bureaucracy and the specific work to be carried out. You should also ask the contact at the host organization specifically about the crime environment in the areas where you will live or be operating. Have members of short-term missionary teams been victimized by criminals? How about full-time missionaries living in the area, or Western tourists? Are there any specific tactics criminals in the area favor? Are there any particular items that should not be brought on the trip?

Other travelers can ask these same questions of friends and family members in the destination country as well as hotels, resorts, tour operators and outfitters.

Travel Advisories and Consular Information Sheets

One of the most important first steps you should take before beginning a trip is to check and see what the U.S. government says about your destination country. A great deal of information can be gleaned from the U.S. government, and travelers should read the consular information sheet and check for travel warnings and public announcements pertaining to their destination countries before embarking on a trip. Such information can be obtained in person at passport agencies inside the United States or at U.S. embassies and consulates abroad. These documents can also be obtained by calling the U.S. State Department, but the quickest and easiest way to obtain them is online — the State Department publishes them all on its website at http://travel.state.gov/.

So, what do all these State Department documents tell us? Well, a "travel warning" is a document recommending that travel to a specific country be deferred or avoided. A "public announcement" is intended to disseminate information about short-term conditions that could pose a risk to American travelers. Public announcements can be issued even when the U.S. government is not sure that Americans will be specifically targeted but is concerned that a potential threat exists. The State Department will often issue public announcements regarding terrorist threats, coups and large public demonstrations, and even noting the coming anniversaries of significant past terrorist events.

The State Department issues travel warnings on only a handful of countries, and many countries do not have any active public announcements pertaining to them, but the department maintains a "consular information sheet" for *every* country, even countries the United States does not have formal diplomatic relations with, such as Iran. The consular information sheet is a useful document that not only tells you what documents you need to enter the destination country but also provides information on crime, safety, security, political stability, in-country medical care, currency regulations and road safety. It also contains contact information for the U.S. embassy and U.S. consulates (if any) in the country. The consular information sheet also usually contains a link to the local U.S. embassy's website.

It is a good idea for travelers to print out a copy of the consular information sheet and take it with them on their trip. At the very least, travelers should be sure to write down the phone number of the U.S. embassy — including the after-hours phone number (which generally rings into the Marine security guard on duty at the embassy's security command center, normally referred to as "Post One," or to the embassy's duty officer.) The paper with the embassy contact numbers should be kept separate from the traveler's wallet, so if the wallet gets lost or stolen the contact information will not be lost with it. The local contact number(s) for the host organization should also be written down on this paper.

One thing to note about consular information sheets is that they generally do not provide advice or security recommendations to travelers. They are intended to provide just the facts, and travelers are then supposed to use the information provided in the consular information sheets to make their own judgments and determine their own courses of action. Because of this, if the consular information sheet for your destination country actually breaks this protocol and does make a recommendation, you should take it seriously.

There is an interesting internal dynamic that goes on when the consular information sheets are written. The embassy's regional security officer (RSO) will normally push to make recommendations and to put as much information about crime and safety as possible into the report. These efforts are normally endorsed by the American Citizen's Services (ACS) unit in the consular section. The RSO and the ACS officers tend to want to include this information and make recommendations to keep people safe because they are the ones who have the most interaction with the victims of such crimes. They are the ones who get called to go out and pick up the pieces after an American has been killed, wounded, raped or kidnapped. Therefore, they want to do whatever they can to avoid these scenarios.

Opposing the efforts of the RSO and ACS officers to publish this type of information are the powerful embassy political and economic sections, which attempt to downplay any reported threats or crime information. Such reporting can affect the host nation's tourism, and tourism equals dollars for the host country government and businesses owned by the nation's ruling elite. In practical terms, a consular information sheet that is seen as "too negative" can make local government officials and influential businessmen angry — and that anger is often conveyed to the embassy's political and economic officers, who try to avoid this situation (and smooth ruffled feathers) by keeping the consular information sheet as bland as possible.

This tension between the embassy's sections is usually decided in favor of the political and economic sections unless there have been several high-profile incidents that have tipped the scale in favor of the RSO and ACS sections, or very good, specific intelligence indicating there is a threat. Therefore, the rule of thumb is that the consular information sheet is normally quite conservative in its portrayal of the dangers present in the destination country. If the dangers do not appear to be downplayed in the consular information sheet, then there is most likely a very real problem in that country.

Other Government Travel Reports

In order to ensure that I am getting a balanced look at a specific country, and to obtain more detailed information, I generally like to look at travel advice from several additional countries — namely, the British, Canadian and Australian governments. The British travel advice website can be found at http://www.fco.gov.uk/, the Canadian at http://www.travel.gc.ca/ and the Australian at http://www.smartraveller.gov.au/.

The U.S. State Department's Bureau of Consular Affairs coordinates daily with the governments of the British, Canadian and Australian governments, so the four countries will have pretty much the same big picture of the security environment in a specific country. It is very unlikely that you would find a U.S. travel advisory warning against travel to country X and then visit the U.K. travel advice site and find the British saying go ahead and visit country X because everything is "just ducky" there.

However, the real value to be gained by reading these different reports is at the granular level. The anecdotal cases the foreign governments discuss in their travel sheets may differ from those contained in the U.S. consular information sheet. For example, when I was compiling a travel briefing for a client recently, I noted in a U.K. advisory that British citizens in a particular city had been victimized by local criminal gangs who had begun to engage in "express kidnappings" — something that the U.S. consular information sheet did not note. Express kidnappings, which are short-term kidnappings meant to drain the contents of the victim's bank account via his or her ATM card, were new for that country, and even though we had seen the tactic used elsewhere in the region, it was helpful to be able to warn our customer of the new threat. So in that case, reading the U.K. advisory in addition to the U.S. consular information sheet was well worth my time.

If your host organization is American, you should also ask if it is a member of the U.S. embassy's warden network. The warden network is an emergency communication system that the U.S. embassy establishes among the American expatriate community in a given country. This network is used to provide warnings of severe crime threats, terrorism threats, civil disturbances, political unrest and natural disasters. It is also used to coordinate the evacuation of American citizens from a particular area, or the entire country, if necessary. The "warden messages" published by the U.S. embassy in a specific country are often posted publicly on the local U.S. embassy website, and are recommended reading for people planning to travel to that country.

Many embassies and consulates also provide additional information about crime and safety on their websites. From the consular information sheet you can find a link to the embassy's website, and that site will usually have links to any consulate websites in that country. Some embassy websites, like the one for the U.S. Embassy in Guatemala, also provide a useful listing of crimes committed against Americans in the country. Travelers should peruse these lists carefully, since they can provide valuable insight into the types of crimes being committed, where the criminals are operating, the types of people they target and the tactics they use. Of course, short-term mission teams should pay particular attention to any crimes against visiting mission teams or Americans in the area where they will be ministering or along the route they will be taking to get there. The same thing goes for tourists: You should pay attention to the types of crime committed against tourists and where they occurred.

Once again, if you read a consular information sheet or warden message and it makes a recommendation, please think very carefully before ignoring the recommendation. While ignoring a recommendation does not mean you will automatically be victimized, the warnings and recommendations are there for a good reason and should be heeded wherever possible. Ignoring them can sometimes lead to terrible consequences. For example, shortly before I arrived in Guatemala, an American missionary family was brutally assaulted on the slopes of a volcano that U.S. government employees were forbidden to visit and that a warden message had warned U.S. citizens against visiting. Then, during my tenure, an American filmmaker was brutally assaulted in a zone of the city that the consular information sheet warned against staying in or even visiting after dark. Also, a missionary was shot after ignoring a recommendation not to drive on the highways outside of the city after dark.

It is also important to remember that conditions in your destination country can change. Because of this, if government travel sites were checked far in advance of the trip, they should be checked a second time shortly before departure to ensure that no critical changes occurred.

Local Laws

When travelers leave the United States, they are no longer subject to U.S. laws and regulations but to the laws of the country they are visiting. Therefore, travelers need to learn as much as they can about those local laws before they travel. This is especially critical for short-term mission teams, because there may be laws against importing evangelistic materials into the destination country or specific rules pertaining to the importation and transportation of medical equipment and medicines. In addition to asking the host organization about these laws, it can also be very useful to check with the destination country's embassy in the United States. A letter from the host country's embassy in the United States explaining who you are and what you are doing, in the local language, can be very useful. Such a letter can help clear bureaucratic obstacles, like customs inspectors, and can be especially useful if a mission team is attempting to bring medicine and medical gear into the country. Such a letter can also be helpful in dealing with government officials who are making threats to impede your mission unless they are bribed.

Travelers should also keep up with the political situation in their destination country and that of the region it is in. Many websites — including that of the company I work for, http://www.stratfor.com — are excellent sources of information pertaining to political, terrorism and security information. General information on the country, its government, culture, customs, etc., can be found at the library or online through any number of websites such as the National Geographic Society and the CIA's World Fact Book. The organization hosting the short-term mission trip could also have interesting and informative material on its website or be able to send you informational packets or DVDs.

The destination country may also have informative government websites, such as a site run by the government department of tourism or the country's embassy in the United States. For obvious reasons, these sites should be read carefully. In most cases, the host country government will want to be as positive as possible to encourage tourism (see my comments above about the ruling elite owning most everything). Therefore, such sites rarely provide any information on crime and security because they fear it could scare tourists (and their dollars) away. If such sites do acknowledge security problems, it is a strong indicator that the problem is too large to ignore and you should pay close attention to any warnings the sites provide.

Health Information

Prior to travel, you should also go the U.S. Centers for Disease Control and Prevention's travel health information site, which can be found at: http://www.cdc.gov/travel/. This site provides a wealth of information about vaccinations required for specific countries and regions, and provides important tips about avoiding insect-borne diseases such as malaria and dengue as well as food- and water-borne ailments such as amoebic dysentery. The CDC also issues travel health precautions and warnings as well as information on sporadic outbreaks of dangerous diseases.

Travelers should also consult with their doctor well in advance of their trip to ensure their vaccinations are up to date and that they have time to receive all the required vaccinations for their destination before they depart. Your doctor can also prescribe anti-malarial medication if required. Even travelers in good health need to ensure they have the appropriate vaccinations and should take measures to avoid contracting dysentery and other food- and water-borne illnesses (it is very difficult to minister to others when you are sick and need to be tended to). Many times travel health clinics will not only give vaccinations but will also issue handy medical travel kits that contain adhesive bandages and an assortment of over-the-counter pharmaceuticals such as pain relievers and anti-diarrhea medicines. Sometimes these kits will even contain prescription antibiotics for use in case of severe dysentery.

Registration and Insurance

It is also prudent for travelers to register with the U.S. State Department before leaving the country. This will be helpful not only in case something happens to you while abroad, or if there is a crisis in the country you are visiting, but also if there is a family emergency in the United States and someone needs to locate you. Registration is free, is accomplished via a secure website and only takes a few minutes. You can register online at: https://step.state.gov/step/.

Another consideration is insurance. You should check your homeowner's insurance policy or call your insurance agent to determine if your property insurance policy will cover losses or theft abroad. It is also prudent to find out if your health insurance will cover you overseas. In many instances, insurance companies will pay for all or a portion of medical coverage overseas, but you will often have to pay for the services at the time they are provided and then get reimbursed by the insurance company once you return home. Therefore, you should ensure that you have a way to pay for any necessary medical treatment. The U.S. embassy can provide assistance in the way of emergency loans to pay for your medical treatment, but such assistance requires a lot of paperwork.

You should also determine whether your medical insurance will pay for the cost of medical evacuation (medevac) in the case of a dire medical emergency. For example, a colleague of mine at the State Department had to be medevaced from Khartoum with cerebral malaria because local medical professionals could not stabilize him and did not have adequate facilities to care for him in Sudan.

In addition, in some countries the medical systems are so poor that even treatment considered routine in the United States should be avoided there at all costs. As part of the security advance team for Secretary of State James Baker's 1991 trip to Albania, I was one of the first Americans to visit the country as communism was fading. At the "premier" hospital in Albania, we found the conditions to be very unsanitary and even learned that the hospital was re-using needles, IV tubing and other medical equipment that is normally used once and thrown away in Western medical facilities. In our report back to headquarters, my partner and I noted that under no circumstances should the secretary be treated in Albania; he should instead be evacuated to Italy or Greece for treatment.

Travelers going to a country with this type of substandard medical care and whose insurance will not pay for medical evacuation should give serious consideration to purchasing a medical insurance policy for the trip that will cover the cost of medical evacuation, which can run into the tens of thousands of dollars. Chances are, you will not need to be medically evacuated, but if you do, the cost of not having the coverage can be staggering.

OSAC: A Great Resource for Organizations

Another great source of information pertaining to overseas security is the U.S. State Department's Overseas Security Advisory Council, or OSAC, which can be found on the Web at: http://www.osac.gov/.

OSAC's website has a lot of useful features and allows you to search for information by country or U.S. diplomatic post. The council also maintains warden messages and crime and safety reports from the various diplomatic posts worldwide. Some of the content on the OSAC site is restricted to OSAC members — called constituents — but much of it is available to the public. You should take the time to read the crime and safety report for your destination country, if it is available.

OSAC membership is designed primarily for corporations with business interests overseas and therefore is not open to individuals. However, any religious, educational or nongovernmental organization that is legally incorporated in the United States can join. I would encourage churches, denominations or other organizations that send a large number of missionaries abroad to join OSAC and take advantage of its benefits.

U.S. Customs: "Know Before You Go"

One other issue you should investigate before leaving the United States is what you can bring back with you. Most people will want to buy souvenirs or mementos to bring home to remember the trip or to give as gifts to family members and friends or, in the case of missionaries, as presents to their sending church and supporters. In addition to obvious items, such as agricultural products and illegal drugs, many other items are prohibited by the U.S. Customs and Border Protection Service.

I learned about these regulations the hard way when I was 17 and returning from a year as an exchange student in Australia. During one of the breaks between trimesters, I had traveled with my anthropology class to spend a week studying an aboriginal tribe in the far north of the country. As part of the tribe's annual adulthood festival, they capture, kill and eat a dugong — the Australian version of a manatee. Dugong were considered an endangered species, but the aborigines were permitted to kill them. I made friends with a tribal elder on the trip who gave me the tusks from the dugong killed for that festival as a souvenir. When I returned to the United States, the customs officers in San Francisco confiscated the tusks when I told them what they were. One of the officers who took them told me I could have been fined or faced criminal charges for attempting to bring in an item that came from an endangered species.

Not all prohibited items are animal-related. Friends who were missionaries in Guatemala and lived in the highlands translating the Scripture into one of the Mayan dialects told me that a friend of theirs in the village where they lived had unearthed a pre-Colombian Mayan artifact while farming. The friend then attempted to give the artifact to the missionaries as a gift. Had the missionaries accepted the item as a gift and tried to bring it back to the United States, they could have faced stiff penalties if caught. Such artifacts are considered part of the Mayan cultural heritage.

The moral of these stories is, in the words of the Customs and Border Protection Service, "Know before you go." Their guide to what you can and cannot bring back into the United States can be found on the Internet at http://www.cbp.gov/xp/cgov/travel/id_visa/kbyg/.

Before-You-Go Checklist

- Send an e-mail or place a call to the host organization asking about security.

- Check the U.S. Department of State travel page for travel advisories and public announcements pertaining to the destination. Read the consular information sheet and print out a copy.

- Check the U.S. Embassy and, if applicable, the local U.S. Consulate websites for additional security information.

- Check the British, Australian and Canadian government travel sites.

- Check the OSAC website for relevant information.

- Register your travel with the U.S. State Department.

- Check with the destination country's embassy in the United States for information pertaining to laws and regulations that could affect your mission. See if they will give you an introductory letter in the native language.

- Check with your doctor. Get required vaccinations. Will he give you a travel first-aid kit?

- Check the CDC site to make sure your doctor doesn't miss any important vaccinations.

- Check your homeowner's insurance to see if it covers theft or losses overseas.

- Check your medical insurance to see if it covers treatment overseas and medevac.

- Review U.S. customs regulations to learn what you can and cannot bring back.

- Check to see if (and which) credit cards are widely accepted in your destination country and city. ATM availability is also important.

CHAPTER THREE:
SITUATIONAL AWARENESS

So then, let us not be like others, who are asleep, but let us be alert and self-controlled.

— 1 Thessalonians 5:6

While criminal and terrorist attacks seem to happen by surprise, it is important to understand that these attacks do not just materialize out of nothingness. In fact, quite the opposite: Criminals and terrorists follow a process when planning their crimes, and this process has several distinct steps: selecting a target, planning the attack, preparing for the attack, launching the attack, escape and exploitation.

This process traditionally has been referred to as the "terrorist planning cycle," but if one looks at it thoughtfully, it becomes apparent that these same steps apply to nearly all crimes. Of course, there will be more time between the completion of the steps in a complex crime like a kidnapping or car bombing than in a simple crime such as purse-snatching or shoplifting. Nevertheless, the same steps are usually followed.

Like any process, this one can be thrown off at various stages, which can affect the outcome of the crime, especially if the criminal is not overly bright and creates a harebrained plan or bungles the execution of an otherwise sound plan. However, in general, once a criminal gets to the execution phase, it is much harder to thwart him than it is earlier in the process. In other words, as a prospective target, your greatest opportunity to throw a monkey wrench into a criminal's plan is in the target selection phase or planning phase, when there are simple actions you can take to make you an unattractive target and, hopefully, divert the criminal to another target.

As part of the target selection phase, every criminal will "size up" his target before attempting to commit a crime. This is called criminal surveillance, or preoperational surveillance. During this time, the criminal will conduct what is essentially a cost/benefit analysis in an effort to determine how much the crime will net, and if he thinks he can escape without being caught. Of course, a terrorist may not view this from a profit motive like a common criminal but instead may consider what kind of media benefit he will get from attacking you, and a suicide bomber is not concerned about escape. Despite these differences, if, in the mind of the criminal, the probable benefit of the crime outweighs the probable cost, the crime will be executed. If the probable cost is too high, or the benefit too little, the criminal will move on to a more favorable target.

All that said, there are two basic ways you can alter this calculation. The first is limiting the valuables you have in your possession (or those you display), which affects the benefit side of the equation. This is a topic we will cover in the next chapter when we discuss what you should *not* take on your trip. The second way to alter the criminal's cost/benefit analysis is by decreasing the criminal's chances of success and increasing his chances of being caught. This is accomplished through preventative security and situational awareness.

Like the rest of the criminal planning process, the amount of time devoted to surveillance will vary depending on the type of crime and the type of criminal involved. A criminal who operates like an ambush predator, such as a purse-snatcher, may lurk in a specific area and lie in wait for a suitable target to come within striking distance. This is akin to a crocodile lying in wait in the watering hole for an animal to come and get a drink. Such a criminal will only have a few seconds to size up the potential target and make that cost/benefit calculation before quickly making his plan, getting ready and striking.

On the other extreme are the criminals who behave more like stalking predators. Such a criminal is like a lion on the savannah, which carefully looks over the herd and selects a vulnerable animal believed to be the easiest to attack. A criminal who operates like a stalking predator, such as a kidnapper or terrorist, may select a suitable target and then take days or even weeks to follow his target, assess its vulnerabilities and determine if the potential take is worth the risk. Normally, such a stalking criminal will prey only on targets he feels certain he can successfully hit, although he will occasionally take more risk for a high-value target.

Of course, there are many other criminals who fall somewhere in the middle. They may take anywhere from a few minutes to several hours to watch a potential target. Regardless of the time spent observing the target, *all criminals will conduct this surveillance, and they are vulnerable to detection during this time* — that is, *if* you are looking for them.

Like the predators we mentioned above, criminals thrive by having the element of surprise on their side. Action is always faster than reaction, and surprise multiplies that differential. Therefore, once a criminal has sprung his trap and begins to execute his plan, it usually means you are within striking range, unless the criminal is inept — and there are some inept criminals out there, but many criminals have had enough practice to become very good at their craft. Therefore, once they attack and catch you by surprise, it's generally too late to completely avoid them, and all you as the target can do is comply with their demands, attempt to escape or fight back — depending on the situation. We will discuss compliance, escape and resistance in detail in a later chapter.

So, if the criminal has the element of surprise as an advantage, you don't have many options. However, when you turn the tables on the criminal and deny him that element of surprise, it is far more difficult for him to launch a successful attack. Because of this, once a criminal has been noticed and has lost his element of surprise, the cost side of the cost/benefit equation climbs dramatically, and the criminal will frequently scrap his plan and divert to an easier target. Criminals, like other predators, clearly prefer easy targets. That is why they prey so frequently on people who are intoxicated, old, heavily distracted or otherwise easy to "get the drop on." Because of this, merely by establishing early eye contact with a potential assailant, you can often ward off an attack, as this small gesture communicates a non-submissive posture without being overtly confrontational. It shows you are not an easy target. (Though remember that in some cultures eye contact may be considered offensive, so it is important to pay attention to your cultural environment.) However, there are a host of other simple, low-key actions such as crossing the street to avoid a possible ambush criminal; walking into a building with security or turning around and quickly walking to a more populated and well-lit area that may be all that is needed to tell a criminal you are on to him.

Several times while shopping in third-world countries, I have observed people attempting to scope me out for a potential pickpocketing or robbery. I also remember a time when my wife and I split up in a market, and when I came back to meet her several minutes later, I saw a guy I am sure was getting ready to try to snatch the fanny pack she kept her money in. In each of these situations, just my making eye contact with the potential thieves deterred them. That type of criminal thrives on surprise, does not desire confrontation, and can be quickly diverted to an easier, less alert victim.

Another time while I was working a low-key protective detail in New York, my partner saw a guy sizing up our female protectee's purse for a snatch. She was talking on her cell phone while walking and not paying any attention to what was going on in the world around her. This made her a perfect mark for a purse snatcher — especially since she was carrying a very expensive designer handbag. Before launching his strike, the criminal gave one last look around, to make sure there were no cops in the area. My partner immediately broke cover as a "discreet" protection agent, made eye contact with him, got his attention and shook his head and said, "No." Shaken by having his purpose identified, the prospective purse-snatcher turned as white as a sheet and rapidly walked away in the other direction. My partner's action had suddenly — and dramatically — altered that criminal's cost/benefit equation.

Mindset

From the examples I just shared, we can see that situational awareness — paying attention to people in your immediate vicinity — is a very useful way to identify potential threats and to provide you with the time required to take proactive measures to avoid a problem. But, in order to gain this awareness, you must first have the proper mindset, because being observant of one's surroundings and of identifying potential threats and dangerous situations is more of an attitude or mindset than it is a hard skill.

The first part of this mindset is recognizing the need to assume responsibility for your own security. As discussed in the first chapter, even Christians need to have a prudent concern for their physical security and should take practical measures to avoid unnecessary risks. Once we have accepted this responsibility we can then proceed to the next component of the mindset, which is having the will to be aware and the discipline to stay that way.

Although situational awareness does require some practice and discipline, it is not a difficult thing to do. It is not something that can only be performed by highly trained counter-surveillance operatives or federal agents. Anyone can practice situational awareness once they have the proper attitude and a little instruction. Now that we've addressed the attitude, let's begin the instruction by discussing the different levels of awareness and identifying which level is the most effective and sustainable for most people.

Levels of Awareness

People typically operate in five distinct levels of awareness. There are several different ways to describe these levels, but for our purposes here I will call these levels "tuned out," "relaxed awareness," "focused awareness," "high alert," and "comatose." Probably the best way I can think of to illustrate the differences between these distinct levels of awareness is to compare them to the different levels of attention we sometimes use while driving.

The first level, tuned out, is like the level of driving I call "autopilot." This is similar to when you are driving in a very familiar environment or are engrossed in thought, a daydream, a song on the radio or even by the kids fighting. Have you ever gotten in the car and arrived somewhere without even really thinking about your drive there? I sometimes do. I also must admit that every once in a while, instead of taking a turn at an intersection to go to the place I am supposed to be going, I find myself going another direction toward a familiar destination like home or church. When I catch myself doing this — or if my wife catches me doing it and I get a "Honey, weren't we supposed to be turning left here?" — I realize that I was tuned out, had my brain set on autopilot and was not really paying attention the way I should have been.

Not only is it easy to drive on autopilot in a familiar area, but the same thing can happen in a strange environment, when we become so engrossed in the new scenery or events happening around us that we completely tune out our driving and the vehicles around us — like a "rubber-necker" who intently stares at an accident on the road and then hits the car in front of him. I can't even begin to tell you how many times I saw that happen on the Beltway when I lived in D.C.!

I liken the second level of awareness, relaxed awareness, to defensive driving. This is a state in which you are relaxed but you are also watching the other cars on the road and are looking for road hazards. If another driver looks like he may not stop at the intersection ahead, you tap your brakes to slow your car in case he does not. Defensive driving does not make you weary and you can drive this way for a long time *if* you have the discipline to keep yourself in the habit. It is really easy to allow yourself to slip into tuned-out mode. Now, if you are practicing defensive driving you can still enjoy the trip, look at the scenery and listen to the radio, but you are not allowing yourself to get so engrossed in those things that they exclude everything else. You are relaxed and having a good time, but you are still watching for road hazards, maintaining a safe following distance and keeping an eye on the behavior of the drivers around you.

The next level of awareness is what I call focused awareness. This is like driving in hazardous road conditions. You need to practice this level of awareness when you are driving on icy or slushy roads — or the terrible pothole- and "chicken bus"-infested roads that exist in many third-world countries. When you are driving in such an environment, you need to keep two hands on the wheel at all times and have your attention totally focused on the road and the other drivers. You don't dare take your eyes off the road or let your attention wander. There is no time for cell phone calls or other distractions. The level of concentration required for this type of driving makes it extremely tiring and stressful. A drive that you normally would not think twice about will totally exhaust you under these conditions because it demands your prolonged concentration and focus.

The third level of awareness is high alert. Watch out! There's a deer in the road! Hit the brakes! This is the level that causes you to get that huge adrenaline rush, pray and gasp for air all at the same time. This happens where that car you were watching doesn't stop at the stop sign and pulls out right in front of you. High alert can be scary, but in this level you are still able to function. You can hit your brakes and keep your car under control. In fact, the adrenalin rush we get in this stage can sometimes even aid our reflexes. But large doses of panic and adrenalin are not good for your health. You can take only small doses of high alert before becoming physically and mentally exhausted.

The last level of awareness, comatose, is what happens when you literally fall asleep at the wheel and cannot respond to stimuli. Aside from sleep, we can become comatose on the other end of the spectrum, if we panic to the point of freezing up. This is the level of awareness where you go into shock, your brain ceases to process information and you simply cannot react to the stimulus. Many times when this happens, a person can go into denial, believing that "this can't be happening to me," or the person can feel like someone observing the event rather than participating in it. Often, time will seem to slow to an absolute crawl and the seconds will stretch out.

Finding the Right Level

Now that we've described the different levels of awareness, what level should we ideally operate in? Our bodies require sleep, so we have to spend several hours each day in the comatose level. When we are sitting at our homes watching a movie or reading a book, it is perfectly alright to operate in the tuned-out mode. However, some people will attempt to maintain the tuned-out mode in decidedly inappropriate environments (e.g., out on the street at night in a third-world slum), or they will maintain a mindset wherein they deny that criminals can victimize them. "It can't happen to me, so there's no need to watch for it." They tune out.

Some people are so tuned out as they go through life that they miss even blatant signs of pending criminal activity directed *specifically at them*. In 1992, I worked an investigation in the Philippines of an American executive who was abducted. While debriefing the man after his rescue, he described in detail how the kidnappers had blocked off his car in traffic and abducted him. Then, to my surprise, he told me that the morning before his abduction, the same group of guys had attempted to abduct him at the exact same location, at the very same time of day and driving the same car! The attackers had failed to adequately box his car in, however, and his driver was able to pull around the blocking vehicle and proceed to the office.

Since the executive did not consider himself to be a potential kidnapping victim, he had just assumed that the incident the day before his abduction was "just another close call in crazy Manila traffic." So, the next morning he took the same route and same car at the same time, and he was nabbed. It was only *after* he had been abducted that he realized that the incident the previous day had been a failed kidnapping attempt. He remarked that there had been something strange about the behavior of guys in the big SUV that tried to block his car that first day, and he felt uneasy with the way they looked at him. He even said that he felt that their driving was strange — even by Manila standards — but he didn't think he would be kidnapped so he didn't really give it a second thought. The executive and his driver had both been tuned out. Unfortunately, the executive paid for this lack of situational awareness by having to withstand an extremely traumatic kidnapping, which included almost being killed in the operation that rescued him.

If you are tuned out when you are driving and something happens, like a deer jumps into the road or a car stops quickly in front of you, you do not see the problem coming. This usually means that you either do not see the hazard in time to avoid it and you hit it, or you totally panic and cannot react to it — either way is not good. These reactions occur because it is very difficult when your mind and body are forced to move quickly from the tuned-out state to the high-alert state. It is like trying to shift your car directly from first gear into fifth, and it stalls. Many times, when people are forced to make this mental jump and they panic (and stall), they go into shock and will actually freeze and be unable to take any action. This is what I call going comatose. This not only happens when we are driving, but it also happens frequently when a criminal catches someone totally unaware and unprepared. Of course, sometimes criminals can catch you when you are driving and unprepared.

One of my former Diplomatic Security Service colleagues experienced this phenomenon first-hand while working a protective detail for the U.S. ambassador in Burundi in 1995. The ambassador decided to join a fact-finding team of foreign observers and local officials who were going to travel to Burundi's Cibitoke province to investigate reports of inter-ethnic violence there. During the trip to the province, the agent, Chris Reilley, was sitting in the right front passenger seat of the ambassador's armored limousine with a local African driver behind the wheel. As the convoy their vehicle was traveling in rounded a turn, the convoy was ambushed by attackers throwing grenades and firing automatic weapons. The driver of the ambassador's limousine panicked, went into shock and froze, stiff as a board. He was comatose — unable to do anything, no matter how loudly Chris yelled at him to get out of the attack zone. After a few seconds, Chris had to reach across the center console of the car, grab the wheel with one hand and use his other hand to press the accelerator so they could escape. Fortunately, Chris' quick action did allow them to escape unharmed. One of my other former colleagues, Larry Salmon, who was driving the embassy's security follow car, and who was the only person in the convoy to return fire at the attackers, was lightly wounded. Larry and Chris both received valor awards for their heroic actions. This story helps demonstrate the dangers inherent in operating in the tuned-out state and how a person can be dramatically shifted into the comatose state by panic. However, being tuned out is not the only hazard: Paranoia is just as dangerous.

I cannot stress enough that situational awareness does not mean being paranoid or obsessively concerned about your security. It does not mean living with the irrational expectation that there is a dangerous criminal lurking around every corner. In fact, we simply cannot operate in a state of focused awareness for extended times, and high alert can only be maintained for very brief periods before exhausting us. The Bible tells us not to worry for a very good reason. Worry and stress wears you out. The "flight or fight" response that God designed us with is very helpful if it can be controlled. However, if it gets out of control, a constant stream of adrenalin and stress is simply not healthy for our bodies or our minds. When we are constantly scared and paranoid, we become mentally and physically burned out. Not only is this dangerous to our physical and mental health, but our security also suffers because it is very hard to be aware of your surroundings when you are a complete basket case. Therefore, being constantly on high alert is not the answer.

So, what we are looking for when we say that you need to practice situational awareness is a level of *relaxed awareness*, a state of mind that can be maintained indefinitely without all the stress associated with focused awareness or high alert. Relaxed awareness is not tiring and allows us to enjoy life and to take time to smell the roses; however, when we do this while practicing relaxed awareness, it means we look for a bee in the rose before placing our nose into it!

The idea is that when you are in an area where there is potential danger, you should go through most of your day in a state of relaxed awareness. Then, if you spot a potential threat, you can "dial yourself up" to a state of focused awareness and take a careful look at that potential threat (and also look for others in the area). If the potential threat proves to be innocuous, and there is nothing to be concerned about, you can dial yourself back down into relaxed awareness and continue on your merry way. If, on the other hand, you look and determine that the potential threat is a probable threat, seeing it in advance allows you to take actions to avoid it. You may never need to elevate up to high alert, since you have avoided the problem. However, once you are in a state of focused awareness you are far better prepared to handle the jump to high alert if the threat does change from potential to actual — if the three guys lurking on the corner do start coming toward you and look as if they are reaching for weapons. The chances of you going comatose are far less if you jump from focused awareness to high alert than if you are caught by surprise and "forced" to go into high alert from tuned out.

Of course, if you know that you must go into an area that is very dangerous, you should dial yourself up to focused awareness when you are in that area. For example, if there is a specific section of highway where a lot of roadblocks are thrown up to stop and rob vehicles, or if there is a part of the city that is controlled (and patrolled) by criminal gangs, it would be prudent to increase your security when you are in those areas. When you depart, you can then go back into relaxed awareness.

Warning Signs of Criminal Behavior

"Okay," you are probably thinking. "I have the right attitude toward security, and I also have the will and discipline to be aware of my environment, but what in the world am I looking for?" We are looking for indications of criminal behavior.

I have a secret to tell you: Criminals are terrible at surveillance and practice terrible surveillance tradecraft. "Tradecraft" is an espionage term that means techniques and procedures, but it also infers quite a bit of finesse. And criminals generally have terrible techniques, use sloppy procedures and lack finesse when they are watching people.

Now, I know I just told you that all criminals conduct pre-operational surveillance. And you would naturally assume that this means they do it well, but just because they do it all the time doesn't mean they are good at it! In fact, most criminals conducting surveillance tend to lurk and look out of place. However, criminals are able to get away with practicing this poor level of tradecraft because most people are not looking for them. These people are not practicing situational awareness.

I can't even begin to tell you how many people I have interviewed after they were victimized who told me they recognized their assailants before the criminals launched their attack. However, many of these people were like that business executive who was kidnapped in the Philippines and did not have the proper mindset — they ignore the potential danger even when they notice something odd, but since they don't act on their observations, they get victimized. When you are interviewing such a person, they usually say something like, "Gee, I thought there was something strange about the behavior of those three guys standing on the corner, but I continued walking anyway and they mugged me."

I remember debriefing an American citizen who had been kidnapped in Guatemala and held until his family paid a sizable ransom. During the debriefing, he told me that he knew the criminals who had kidnapped him had surveilled his morning routine by sending two people to pretend to be lovers and sit on a bench in a park down the street from his home. He said that he knew there was something wrong with the way the couple behaved when he passed by and looked at them, but he couldn't put his finger on it. Unfortunately, he had a lot of time to think about that couple when he was being held hostage.

This awkward or abnormal behavior that criminals often exhibit when they are watching us is what we call in surveillance terms "bad demeanor." The behavior a person needs to master the art of surveillance tradecraft, good demeanor, is not intuitive. In fact, the things one has to do to maintain good demeanor frequently run counter to human nature. Because of this, intelligence and security professionals who work surveillance operations receive extensive training that includes many hours of heavily critiqued practical exercises, often followed by field training with a team of experienced surveillance professionals. This training teaches and reinforces good demeanor. Criminals and terrorists do not receive this type of training and, as a result, bad surveillance tradecraft has long proven to be an Achilles' heel to terrorist and criminal organizations.

Believe it or not, surveillance is an unnatural activity, and a person doing it must deal with strong feelings of self-consciousness and of being out of place. Because of this, people conducting surveillance frequently suffer from what is called the "burn syndrome" — the erroneous belief that the person he is watching has spotted him. Feeling "burned" will cause the person conducting the surveillance to do unnatural things, such as suddenly ducking back into a doorway or turning around abruptly when he unexpectedly comes face to face with his target. People inexperienced in the art of surveillance find it difficult to control this natural reaction. Even experienced surveillance operatives occasionally have the feeling of being burned; the difference is they have received a lot of training and they are better able to control their reaction and work through it. They are able to maintain a normal looking demeanor while their insides are screaming, "Oh, no! The person I'm watching has seen me!"

I have conducted surveillance on many criminal suspects. Some of the operations lasted for weeks, and some of the people I was watching even practiced some crude form of surveillance detection. Many times during these surveillance operations I was certain that my target had seen me — I felt burned. However, I was always surprised when it came time to arrest my suspect. I would meet the person face to face and they wouldn't recognize me, even though I was *certain* they had burned me while I was watching them.

In addition to doing something stupid when they feel burned, another very common mistake amateurs make when conducting surveillance is the failure to get into proper "character" for the job or, when in character, appearing in places or carrying out activities that are incongruent with the character's "costume." The terms used to describe these role-playing aspects of surveillance are "cover for status" and "cover for action." Cover for status is a person's purported identity — their costume. They can pretend to be a student, a businessman, a repair man, etc. Cover for action explains why that person is doing what they are doing — why has that guy been standing on that street corner for a half hour?

The purpose of using good cover for action and cover for status is to make the presence of the person conducting the surveillance look routine and normal. When done right, the operative fits in with the mental snapshot subconsciously taken by the target as he goes about his business. Frequently, inexperienced people who conduct surveillance do not use good cover for action or cover for status, and they can be easily detected.

An example of bad cover for status would be someone dressed as a businessman walking in the woods or at the beach. An example of bad cover for action is someone pretending to be sitting at a bus stop who remains at that bus stop even when the bus for that route has passed. But most criminals conducting surveillance practice no cover for action or cover for status. They just lurk and look totally out of place.

In addition to plain old lurking, other giveaways include moving when the target moves, communicating when the target moves, avoiding eye contact with the target, making sudden turns or stops, or even using hand signals to communicate with other members of a surveillance team or criminal gang. They also can tip off the person they are watching by entering or leaving a building immediately after the person they are watching or simply by running in street clothes. Sometimes, people who are experiencing the burn syndrome exhibit almost imperceptible behaviors that you sense more than observe. It may not be something you can articulate, but you just know there was something wrong or odd about the way that person behaved. People who are not watching you usually do not exhibit this behavior.

The U.S. government uses an acronym to teach people what bad surveillance looks like: TEDD. That stands for time, environment, distance and demeanor. The idea is that if you see someone repeatedly over time, in different environments or from a distance, you are under surveillance. You might see a stalking predator repeatedly over time and distance and in different environments, but you are not likely to see an ambush predator that way. Therefore, when we are talking about criminal surveillance, demeanor is the most critical of the four elements.

The mistakes criminals make while conducting surveillance can be quite easy to catch — as long as someone is looking for them. If no one is looking, however, hostile surveillance is remarkably easy. This is why terrorist groups and criminals have been able to get away with conducting surveillance for so long using inexperienced surveillants who practice poor tradecraft. This is also why we need to practice situational awareness. It works!

The Flip Side of Situational Awareness

One of the things that I always encourage my surveillance and countersurveillance students to do is to become a student of people. To watch them and, based solely on observations, attempt to figure out who they are and what their story is. In other words, to attempt to decipher their cover for status and cover for action — why they are there and what they are doing.

Studying people will not only allow you to pick up on demeanor mistakes. More important for us as Christians, practicing relaxed awareness and paying attention to the people around us also opens up a whole new world of ministry opportunities for us. It allows us to "tune in" to other people and to perceive things we would miss if we were self-absorbed or just tuned out. In other words, it affords us an excellent opportunity to look at the needs and burdens of other people.

Therefore, when all is said and done, in many ways situational awareness allows us to be more Christ-like in the way we view the world.

CHAPTER FOUR:
PREPARING FOR THE TRIP

Your beauty should not come from outward adornment, such as braided hair and the wearing of gold jewelry and fine clothes. Instead, it should be that of your inner self, the unfading beauty of a gentle and quiet spirit, which is of great worth in God's sight.

— 1 Peter 3:3-4

There are many fine handbooks and travel guides that talk about what you should bring with you on an overseas trip. The excellent advice they provide should be heeded. However, from my experience, the crucial issue from a security standpoint is not so much what you should bring with you, but rather what you should *not*. Quite frequently, travelers bring unnecessary items with them on trips that attract the attention of potential criminals and/or cause them considerable angst when the items are lost or stolen.

In the last chapter we talked about the cost/benefit equation that criminals consider and how what you have (or what you show to criminals) can have a significant impact on the benefit side of that equation. Simply put, a criminal is willing to take far more risk to get a $3,000 Rolex than a $30 Timex.

Most Americans do not consider themselves wealthy, but when we compare our standard of living to that of someone in the third world, the difference is night and day. Even a plane ticket to visit a place like Haiti from the United States can cost several times the annual per capita income in Haiti, which is only about $450. Furthermore, per capita income estimates do not account for the very wealthy citizens in a country, so because there are a few very wealthy citizens in such countries who make many times that amount, there are many, many people who make less than that per capita income figure. Most of us who can afford to travel overseas, whether on a mission trip or a vacation, have a standard of living that only the very rich in our destination country can attain. In other words your watch, smartphone, laptop and even your sunglasses may be worth more money than some of the people you will encounter during your trip make in an entire year. It is important to remember that when you are in a third-world country, items that you would not think twice about carrying in the U.S. might very easily draw the attention of criminals.

It is also important to understand that a display of wealth will influence not only how criminals view us, but also how we are viewed by the people we are seeking to minister to — ostentatious displays of wealth can cause a rift that is very difficult to overcome. Therefore, based on both of these considerations, we should endeavor to minimize what we take with us. With this in mind then, the first rule to remember as you prepare for your trip is simply this: *Try not to take anything with you that will draw undue attention to yourself.*

The second rule is equally important: *Do not take anything with you that you are not prepared to lose.* This is not only because there are some things that are impossible to replace should they be lost or stolen — such as your grandmother's engagement ring or your father's gold watch — but because the emotional attachment you have to such objects may cause you to make irrational decisions if you are faced with the loss of the object. We will discuss this in much more detail in the chapter on dealing with threats, but I think it is worth repeating here that there is no object, no matter how expensive or emotionally significant, that is worth losing your life over — or the life of someone you are traveling with. Of course, as noted in Chapter Three, our ideal is to practice situational awareness, see potential threats before they can surprise us and then avoid them. However, there are times when we can be surprised by criminals who succeed in getting the drop on us for whatever reason, and if that is the case, we must react accordingly.

In many places, criminals are just interested in getting the goods and getting away. They are not interested in gratuitous violence, but at the same time, they will not hesitate to shoot or stab you should you resist. If you give them the goods they are demanding, they will quite often go their merry way and not harm you. Unfortunately, when I was serving in Guatemala, several American citizens resisted robbery attempts and paid for their resistance by being beaten, shot, stabbed, and in a few cases, even killed.

Of course there are places and cultures where gratuitous violence is the norm, and those places require special attention and greater security measures. However, in general, if you leave precious items at home you remove the possibility that they will attract a criminal and you will not face the temptation to refuse to surrender them if you are threatened.

In light of these two rules, let's discuss in detail how to minimize the risk posed by the items you will carry on your trip.

Wallets, Cash and Credit Cards

The first thing I want to discuss is your wallet. This is because quite frankly, most people carry far more in their wallets than they need to — or should. In fact, many people are not even aware of everything that is in their wallets. There is a current commercial for the Capital One credit card that has the tag line, "What's in Your Wallet?" Unfortunately, many people cannot answer this simple question. Honestly, if your wallet were stolen right this minute, could you make a detailed list of everything that is in it? Would you be able to quickly notify your bank and credit card companies of the theft? If not, read on; this section is for you.

There are people I know who have wallets several inches thick, and I am not talking just about women; we men are just as guilty. Such a wallet is, unfortunately, a criminal's treasure trove. Not only can criminals benefit from whatever cash and credit cards are in that wallet, but they can also frequently get enough information to do far more substantial damage to your bank account.

This is especially true in cases where people keep credit card and ATM PIN numbers written in their wallets. If a criminal gets your wallet and he gets his hands on your credit and ATM cards, why make his life any easier by providing the PINs, too? Please don't write PIN numbers down.

To compound this problem, many people will also have their bank account numbers listed in the wallet (or have a check with the account number on it) and people, as creatures of habit, tend to use the same PIN numbers for multiple accounts. Please do not use the same PIN numbers for multiple uses, especially sensitive things like banking and credit cards.

People also frequently make the mistake of keeping their Social Security cards in their wallets. The Social Security card is a document that, along with your driver's license — which will in all likelihood be in your wallet — could allow someone to easily assume your identity. This crime is far worse than a simple theft. It is a crime that can cause victims years of legal anguish.

During my years as a DSS agent, I worked countless passport fraud cases, and in most of these cases the people attempting to commit the fraud assumed the identity of someone else. In some cases, the person assuming the identity purchased the identity documents from a drug user or other criminal, but in other cases, the identity came from an unsuspecting victim. It broke my heart to listen to stories of people who had their credit ruined due to such fraud. One poor guy even had his driver license revoked and faced many hundreds of dollars of fines and an arrest warrant for unpaid traffic citations because of the actions of the person who had assumed his identity and been issued a driver's license in his name. Identity fraud is a serious problem.

If you need to show your Social Security card for some reason, like starting a new job, do so, but then take the card home and leave it in a secure location. You should also be careful not to write your Social Security number down in your wallet. Instead, you should memorize and safeguard it. Your Social Security number could allow an imposter to get loans, credit cards and bank loans in your name. Years ago, when I was in the Army, we used to have our Social Security numbers printed on our checks so we could use them at the PX and Commissary. This was a *terrible* idea and a case of identity fraud waiting to happen! So, if you have your Social Security card in your wallet, take it out of there and lock it up in a safe, fireproof location at home. For all the above mentioned reasons, those little metal Social Security card replicas with your number engraved on them are also terrible to carry.

What, then, do you need in your wallet for an overseas trip? One thing is your health insurance card. Another is your driver's license if you are going to drive, though obtaining an international driving permit is a good idea if it is accepted in the country you are traveling to in lieu of your U.S. license — especially countries where authorities may not be able to read your English-language license. If you're not going to drive abroad, simply leave your driver's license at home — it is one less thing to replace if your wallet is stolen, and your passport is the only identity document you really need to travel.

As far as credit cards go, you should carry no more than two and maybe an ATM card. One of the two credit cards should be a Visa or MasterCard, and the second can be another card such as an American Express Card or Discover (though a Visa and a MasterCard is also a good combination.) It is important that you learn in advance which cards are accepted in your destination country before you leave.

If there are not many ATMs in your destination country or city, or if you have a credit card that allows you to take cash advances from an ATM, you should consider leaving your ATM card at home. Why carry (and potentially lose) something you can't use or don't need? If you do decide to take an ATM card, you should ensure that the account your ATM card is connected to only has a limited amount of cash in it (like your checking account) and not your entire life savings. If you are the victim of an express kidnapping, your abductors will likely keep you until the account linked to your ATM card has been drained. They have been known to keep victims locked in car trunks for days in order to drain the account linked to the ATM card.

One other thing you will need to do is make is a list of the card numbers of the credit/ATM cards you are taking with you and the phone number for reporting a stolen card to each of your credit card companies. Make sure that the phone number will work outside the United States. In many instances, the toll-free numbers listed on the back of a credit card to report a lost or stolen card will not work from overseas locations, so you will need to find a number that can be dialed from overseas. You should also write down the numbers of any traveler's checks you are talking with you and the contact number to report lost or stolen checks on this same list. (In the world of credit cards, traveler's checks are becoming increasingly hard to use, so make sure they are accepted in your destination country before purchasing them.) Take one copy of this information with you on your trip, but keep it separate from your wallet so you won't lose it if your wallet gets lost or stolen. Since it has credit card numbers on it, it is sensitive, so guard it carefully. Do not include the card security code number (sometimes also called the card verification code or card verification value) on this list. The combination of the card number and the security code could allow someone who steals or finds your paper to use your card to charge things. Leave another copy of this information in a safe place back home with someone who you can call in case you lose your copy of the list in addition to your wallet.

And while we are speaking of wallets, I believe personally it is a very bad idea for men to carry theirs in their back pockets. Even in the U.S. I carry a front-pocket wallet and money clip — I always thought it would be terribly embarrassing for a so-called security expert to get pickpocketed. Front pocket wallets or money clips are far harder for a pickpocket to get to than a wallet kept in a back pants pocket. Women should also consider foregoing their normally large wallets for their trip and carry a smaller billfold.

It is also an excellent idea to divide up your money into different bundles — one bundle with large bills and another bundle with your smaller, spending cash. You should then keep these two bundles in different pockets or places on your body. That way, people watching you pull out a wad of bill to purchase something will not be able to see your large bills. I personally keep my spending money in my left front pocket and my larger bills in my right front pocket, but large bills can also be kept in other secure places like an ankle pouch or a pouch under your shirt. Also, if a thief sees you pull money out of your left front pocket to buy things, he will consider it logical for you to pull that same wad out and hand it to him if he robs you.

I also try to keep my credit cards in a separate bundle with the hope that any potential thief would be happy with the small bills wad and leave my credit cards and large bills in peace. I would also attempt to give up my big bills separately from the credit cards if a thief insists on more than my small bills, but generally I try to ensure that I have enough in the small bills wad to keep a thief happy without allowing them to hit the jackpot. Couples traveling together should consider dividing their money and credit cards between them so that if one is victimized or loses something, the other will have some cash.

Obviously, if confronted by a thief the objective is to try to get the thief to take as little as possible and leave you alone. However, if the thief is not satisfied with the spending money wad, give up the big bills and even the credit cards if forced to. Again, the cash is not worth getting hurt or killed for.

Leave all your club membership cards and other unnecessary wallet clutter at home. They will not do you much good overseas and could even get you into trouble. Consider the case of Charles Hegna, a U.S. Agency for International Development employee and an accountant, who was killed during the 1984 hijacking of Kuwait Airways flight 221. Mr. Hegna reportedly had a card in his wallet that identified him as a Certified International Accountant (an organization whose initials were "CIA.") In combination with Mr. Hegna's official passport the "CIA card" reportedly brought Mr. Hegna to the attention of the hijackers and he was the first American to be executed during the hijacking ordeal.

I also know of a case in Mexico in which an individual was the victim of an express kidnapping while on vacation. He was the CEO of a company and had business cards in his wallet noting such. When the criminals examined the victim's wallet, they unexpectedly found themselves with a big fish, and they then decided to hold him for a far larger ransom than just the contents of his ATM-linked checking account. Because of a business card, the man's short-term express kidnapping was turned into a much longer — and far more costly — ordeal. If you are on vacation or on a mission trip, there really is no need for cards that indicate you are a CEO or bank president. Also remove any reserve, military or other identification cards or even humorous cards (like a "terrorist hunting license") in your wallet that you do not absolutely need for the trip. Such things could come back to haunt you.

Now, not all thieves are in the third world, and we have plenty of them in the United States. I would therefore encourage you to consider implementing many of these wallet suggestions in the United States, too — especially knowing what is in your wallet, minimizing what you carry, and not carrying Social Security cards and PIN numbers.

Other Items

Sunglasses — Instead of the expensive Ray-Ban, Oakley or Maui Jim sunglasses, consider getting a cheap pair of sunglasses. You can get glasses that will protect your eyes from UV light for less than $20.

Jewelry — Chains, earrings, rings. Is there really any need for you to wear that thick gold chain or large dangling earrings? Both of these items (like sunglasses and cameras) are very tempting for snatch and grab criminals. I know a woman whose ear lobe was ripped open when a criminal on the back of a moped snatched a dangling gold earring from her ear.

Wedding rings — These are often good to have, especially for a woman looking to avoid any unwanted attention from the opposite sex. However, if you have a large, expensive band with diamonds or other precious stones, or a band with a lot of sentimental value, you might want to seriously consider buying a plain band to wear instead. You should also leave your diamond engagement ring and other rings at home.

Cameras — Unless you are a professional photographer, you might want to consider whether you really need to carry that very expensive camera on your trip. If you do decide to take it with you, make sure you back up any important photos that may be on the memory card. You should also check to see if the theft or loss of the camera will be covered on your homeowner's insurance policy.

Purses — Like wallets, purses can be real treasure troves for thieves. Carefully review your purse to see what is in it and, like your wallet, weed out all the unnecessary items. Thieves will commonly slit a purse strap (like a camera strap) and take it or just try to grab it and run. I have also encountered many cases where purses and backpacks were slit open with a razor blade and their contents removed. I normally recommend that if women really think they need a purse, they take a small purse that can be clutched tightly to the front of their body or they take a fanny pack for all their little necessary items. Purses and backpacks are natural targets for thieves, and women should seriously consider placing their important things in their front pockets or placing them in an ankle or inside-the-shirt pouch. If you carry a purse or fanny pack, do not lay it on the floor in a restaurant or hang it on the back of your chair.

Travel documents — When you handle your passport think to yourself that you are handling a wad of $100 bills, because you are. On the black market, a stolen, genuine U.S. passport can fetch up to several thousand dollars. You should make a couple of photocopies of your passport. If you have a safe place to keep your real passport, do so and carry the copy on your person (if that is legal in the country you are to visit). The other copy should be kept with the trusted contact who has your credit card information so that you can refer to it in case your real passport and the copy you carry on you are lost — don't laugh, it happens. If you are a trip leader and have collected the passports for your entire team for safekeeping, that bag or box you now hold in your hands is worth tens of thousands of dollars — a small treasure — and should be safeguarded accordingly.

Clothing — Be really careful what you wear. Make sure that you do not wear clothing that is considered immodest by the local culture or t-shirts with sayings that might be considered offensive. If possible, attempt to wear clothing that is generic or neutral and does not readily identify you as an American.

Electronics

Laptops, tablets, iPods and cell phones can in many ways serve as de facto electronic wallets. Again, do you know what's in yours? The old American Express commercial used to warn travelers, "Don't leave home without it." In today's world, many travelers find it hard to leave home without at least a laptop, cell phone and tablet or e-reader. Some also tote iPods in which sensitive information has been stored.

Laptops and other electronic devices have become essential travel accessories because of the vast amount of information they can hold in a relatively small space. For this reason, they — or just the information they contain — make a prize catch for anyone with hostile intentions. Travelers should take precautions to not only physically safeguard these devices but also the information they contain. This allows you to mitigate the potential adverse effects of a compromise and can save you from a serious headache. While the loss of a laptop is bad, the loss of the information on it can be even worse if identity or financial thieves can use that information.

The best way to protect sensitive information contained in a laptop, phone or tablet is, obviously, to avoid exposing the device to potentially compromising situations. Leave it at home. But if you find the need to take such items abroad, you need to do the same thing to them that we just did with wallets and purses — minimizing the amount of sensitive information stored on the computer. If at all possible, the electronic devices you take with you overseas should contain only information that is specific to current trip. That way, should the device be compromised, you can take some small comfort in knowing that all of your sensitive information is not in the hands of the thieves. If you used your laptop to fill out your income tax return last year and have the return saved on the drive, a criminal can get an incredible amount of personal information, such as bank account numbers and Social Security numbers. Aside from minimizing what data you take with you, it is also prudent to ensure that all important data on the electronic devices you take on a trip is backed up in another location.

Criminals like electronic items like laptops and tablets because of their high value on the resale market. These devices are frequently stolen in airports, hotel lobbies and restaurants, on trains and buses, and even in the street. Therefore, a laptop should never be set down in a place where a thief can quickly snatch it and run. In addition, it is a good idea to carry a laptop in a non-typical bag, rather than its case, which often has the manufacturer's logo on it and screams "steal me, I'm expensive."

If you really need to take your laptop, phone or tablet, you should obviously employ any security features the device has, such as requiring a password to access the device. You should also give serious consideration to using a commercially available encryption program to encrypt the important information stored on the device and help protect your information from theft. If you need to store user names, account numbers and PINs in your tablet, laptop, or phone, there are very reasonable or even free encrypted password vaults that can be used to protect your usernames, passwords and pins. Such a program allows you to protect all your passwords and pins while only having to remember one password. When installed on an encrypted hard drive, these programs give you a second layer of security. But, obviously, make sure your passwords to your encrypted hard drive and password vaults are very robust and conform to good password protocols — that they are at least 8 or 10 characters long and include capital letters, numbers and symbols. I personally like to use groups of words numbers and symbols that are more than 20 characters long.

In high-crime areas it is advisable to carry the laptop's hard drive separately from the rest of the computer, such as in a coat pocket or in your suitcase or garment bag with your clothes. An alternate suggestion is to carry your data on a removable USB memory stick and not on the computer itself. Then, should the laptop be stolen, the thief will not get the data — which likely is much more valuable to you than the machine itself.

CHAPTER FIVE:
SECURITY AT THE AIRPORT
AND IN THE AIR

If I go up to the heavens, you are there; if I make my bed in the depths, you are there. If I rise on the wings of the dawn, if I settle on the far side of the sea, even there your hand will guide me, your right hand will hold me fast.

— Psalm 139:8-10

The Terrorist Threat

When thinking about air travel security, most people automatically focus on hijacking and airline bombings. Certainly those things are scary and spectacular, but they are very, very uncommon — especially in the post-9/11 era of airline security. Travelers are far more likely to be victimized at the airport than they are while on an aircraft, and odds are a criminal and not a terrorist will target them. But we will talk about both the criminal and terrorist threats and security on aircraft as well as in airports.

Terrorists choose to strike airports and airliners because of their symbolism and the fact that any attack against them will be certain to drive a lot of media coverage. Remember that terrorism is propaganda by deed, and that the end goal of most terrorists is not to kill people as much as it is to get publicity. Publicity is larger and more important than death. Aircraft are also ideal terrorist targets, because in an aircraft you can have hundreds of people who are thousands of feet up in the air. They are tightly packed together in a pressurized tube and very vulnerable to an attack.

Although al Qaeda and its jihadist progeny have demonstrated a continued focus on targeting aircraft, security enhancements have made it very difficult to conduct an attack against an airplane. We have only seen two aircraft destroyed in bombing attacks since 9/11, and those were taken down on Aug. 24, 2004, by a twin suicide bombing attack committed by Chechen "black widow" female suicide bombers. There have been a couple of close calls, like the botched Dec. 22, 2001, shoe bombing attack and the failed Christmas Day 2009 underwear bomb attack, but most plots to attack aircraft, like the 2006 liquid bomb plot in the United Kingdom, are thwarted before they get to the operational stage.

Security has adapted to the three modes of attack represented by the shoe bomb, the underwear bomb and the liquid bomb plot. Passengers now have to take their shoes off, they are not permitted to take large containers of liquid into the cabin, and body scanners look for underwear bombs. However, it is important to recognize that as long as there are passengers and luggage on aircraft, there will always be ways creative bomb-makers can smuggle explosives on board. For this reason, it is very important for airline crews and passengers to practice good situational awareness.

In both the shoe bomb and underwear bomb plots, passengers interviewed after the fact reported that they noticed the bombers behaving abnormally. Had they reported this behavior to the crew, there is a good chance that the plots could have been thwarted before the attackers attempted to ignite their devices. Both plots failed when the devices failed to ignite. Had these devices exploded, the passengers sitting near them would have likely been killed, and there is a good chance the planes would have been destroyed. Certainly no one wants to be a chicken little and make a false warning, and there are harmless people on aircraft that are nervous fliers, emotionally distraught or perhaps a plain old strange, but pointing out suspicious behavior to a member of the crew can be done in a very low-key manner. The crewmember can investigate and perhaps confirm your suspicions, or maybe even pass the information on to an Air Marshal if there is one aboard your flight.

Is there a group of individuals who appears to be behaving unnaturally, or who appear to be scheming something? Remember, this is not intended to induce paranoia or Islamophobia, but if you have a group of fit young guys communicating together and giving off demeanor signals that they are up to no good, you should obviously point them out to your aircrew. Likewise, if you see an individual who is extremely nervous, is fidgeting and sweating profusely, you should discreetly point that person out to a member of the aircrew.

A second factor that has helped to mitigate the threat of a 9/11-style attack has been a change in the mentality of aircrews and the flying public. When I was an agent, I used to travel armed all over the country and all over the world. One of the requirements we had for doing so was to attend an annual briefing by the Federal Aviation Administration

(FAA). In these briefings we were always urged not to intervene in a hijacking event because the conventional wisdom was that hijackers were going to land the plane and then either surrender or be taken out by a professional take-down team from either Delta Force or the SEALS. Of course the 9/11 attacks changed that mindset. Even on Sept. 11, 2001, the passengers and crew of United Flight 93 fought back to take control of their aircraft and prevent it from being used as a guided cruise missile.

Another part of the old mindset is that in security briefings, we as agents were always advised to sit against the windows, so that in case of a hijacking, we were further away from the aisle and it would be farther for the hijackers to reach to strike us or to immediately grab us if they wanted to kill a hostage to send a message. In the new paradigm, I want to sit on the aisle so that I can help lead other passengers in an attack on the hijackers if I am ever caught in that situation. I always travel with a small aluminum flashlight and a heavy metal pen in my briefcase and always keep my briefcase under the seat in front of me. They can be used as striking weapons in case it is necessary to intervene.

In an attack on a plane, or even in an accident, fire can be a killer. Fire is dangerous on an aircraft because of the oxygen-rich environment, the sensitive nature of avionics controls and the presence of thousands of gallons of fuel aboard the plane. Another significant danger is all the plastic and other materials used to manufacture aircraft. When they burn, they can produce a heavy cloud of toxic smoke. Because of this, historically more victims in aircraft accidents have been killed by smoke inhalation than by the impact of the crash itself. I also like to sit in or near an exit row to make my route to the exit as short as possible in case of an emergency.

I also recommend that travelers carry a smoke hood in their carry-on luggage. A smoke hood is a protective device that fits over the head and provides protection from smoke inhalation. It also provides protection from the smoke for the wearer's eyes. Smoke hoods are relatively inexpensive devices that can be carried in a briefcase or purse and quickly donned in case of emergency. They will usually provide around 20-30 minutes of breathing time — which could quite literally mean the difference between life and death in a smoke-filled aircraft. While there are oxygen systems in aircraft, such systems are designed for use in a cabin depressurization emergency and not a fire. In fact, in a cabin fire, the activation of the oxygen system and the addition of all that extra oxygen to the air could dramatically increase the intensity of the fire. Besides, the oxygen masks are fixed to the bulkhead above your seat and cannot help you get out of the plane when it is time to evacuate. A smoke hood will go with you and facilitate your evacuation. This is why FAA regulations require smoke hoods for flight and cabin crews — though not for passengers. This stems from economic factors and does not reflect on the utility of the smoke hoods. In most corporate aviation and in high-priced fractional ownership aircraft, there is a smoke hood on board for each passenger.

I have two caveats regarding smoke hoods. First, ensure that any smoke hood you buy is capable of filtering out dangerous carbon monoxide. Some smoke hoods are not. Second, ensure that you purchase a smoke hood that operates using a filter and not a system based upon a compressed oxygen cartridge. Even though some aircrews use compressed oxygen cartridge smoke hoods, and they will protect you from carbon monoxide and dangerous gases, the Transportation Safety Administration will not allow passengers to carry items with compressed oxygen cartridges aboard aircraft.

If the plane were to crash in the dark, the combination of the smoke hood with a small flashlight could save your life. This equipment combination is also very helpful in the event of a bus or subway fire, or even a fire in your hotel or mission center.

The improvements in airline security have also resulted in a shift of terrorist targeting. Airports are divided into two general parts: the area outside the security checkpoint and the area behind the security checkpoint. In recent years, some terrorists decided that since it is too difficult to get weapons through security at the airport and aboard an aircraft, they would just attack targets outside the secure area. This trend was seen in the Jan. 24, 2011, suicide bombing at Moscow's Domodedovo Airport, the June 30, 2007, failed suicide bombing attack against the international airport in Glasgow, Scotland, and the March 2, 2011, attack against U.S. airmen at the airport in Frankfurt, Germany.

Because of this, time spent in line at the ticket counter or at other places outside of the airport's secure area should be minimized as much as possible. If you are able to check in for your flight at home and print out your boarding passes in advance, you should consider doing so. When you cannot use advance check-in for an international flight, you should plan to arrive at the ticket counter early to avoid the really long lines that can cause you to wait for hours on the non-secure side of the airport. The lines can be especially long in airports overseas.

Knowing airline safety regulations about what you can and cannot take on board an aircraft and coming to the airport prepared to comply with them can also help expedite getting through the security checkpoints and into the secure side of the airport. If you are hungry, need to use the restroom or want to do some souvenir shopping, you should take care of those things before you get to the airport or wait and stop into an airport café, restroom or duty free shop after you have passed through security.

The Criminal Threat

Terrorism is not the only threat that faces air travelers, however. There are also concerns about crime. Like the rest of the public, criminals travel, too. Yet people are often quite careless with their belongings while they are aboard an aircraft. I can't even count the number of people who have left their purses and briefcases unattended next to me while they went to use the restroom during a flight. In such a scenario it would be very easy for a criminal to quickly rifle through the bag and snatch your valuables. It would be very troubling to land at an airport and then find your wallet gone as you went to exchange money or your passport gone as you attempted to pass through immigration. Because of this, you should ask a known, trusted companion to keep an eye on your bag if you get up to use the restroom. If you are traveling alone you should take your purse of briefcase with you into the restroom. Yes, airline restrooms are cramped and dirty, but a little inconvenience is better than losing your wallet or passport.

Despite the high level of security normally associated with airports, a lot of crime occurs at or around them. In fact, criminals victimize far more travelers every year than terrorists do. The crime problem at airports stems primarily from the fact that airports present a large concentration of potential victims in one place. This is compounded by the fact that most travelers carry things worth stealing, such as money, jewelry, cameras and electronic equipment. Furthermore, many times travelers are exhausted, unfamiliar with the place and culture, and groggy or perhaps even a little tipsy after a long international flight. In other words, many travelers in airports are not practicing good situational awareness. This makes an airport a target-rich environment for criminals.

Due to the criminal threat, passengers should not rely solely on airport security for their personal protection. Instead they must take responsibility for their own security, and the first step in doing so is recognizing that airports are a prime habitat for criminals.

As with the terrorist threat, the airport security barrier makes it more difficult for criminals wanting to target travelers to get to the secure, or "hard," side of the airport without boarding passes or airport identification — or to get out after they've committed a crime. Because of this, much more theft happens on the unsecure side than on the hard side. However, that does not mean the secure side of the airport is safe from criminals or that you can let your guard down. Crime occurs on the hard side of the airport every day. Purses, briefcases and laptop bags are especially sought, and you should never hang them on the back of your chair or set them down in a place beside or under your table where they can be easily snatched.

We've previously talked about minimizing the time you spend outside of security at the airport you are departing from, but it is also advisable to minimize the time spent on the non-secure side of the airport at your destination. This means travelers should retrieve their bags and leave the airport as quickly as possible. If you are traveling with checked luggage, be very careful that you do not set your laptop, briefcase or other carry-on bag down on the floor as you retrieve your checked bags from the luggage carousel. If you must set such items down, try to stand on the shoulder strap, or have a trusted companion watch them. If there is tight security in the baggage claim area, you can be a little more relaxed, but if there is little or no security there, you should be very careful. Even though the baggage claim is usually behind customs and immigration in most countries, bags still can be — and are — stolen there, so pay attention.

Once you have cleared customs and immigration, do not mill around in the arrival hall area. If you can do so, try to collect all the people traveling with you in the secure area before you go out into the arrival hall, where there are often large crowds waiting to receive passengers and where criminals and pickpockets use the press of the crowd to screen their activities. Criminals often use this area to identify potential victims. It is an easy place for a criminal to lurk for hours unnoticed as long as he looks like a taxi driver or a person waiting to pick someone up from the airport. Such lurking criminals are looking for people who seem to have money or other things worth stealing and who are lost, confused and unsure of where they are going. Many times they will offer victims a discounted taxi fare to their destination, but instead take them to a location where they can be robbed or even kidnapped by armed accomplices.

Because of this, if at all possible, travelers should attempt to arrange transportation to their hotel or mission center in advance. Often hotels will provide shuttle buses or have established transportation arrangements with the more reliable taxi companies. The hotels have a vested interest in keeping their guests safe, so they try to take good care of you. In the third world, taxi drivers are not as well monitored as they are in the United States, and there are frequent instances in the third world of taxi drivers robbing their passengers, setting their passengers up to be robbed or kidnapped, or stealing from passengers by running up the fare. Travelers should never accept a ride from maverick taxi drivers who solicit them in the arrival hall or at the airport exit. If travelers must take a taxi from a company they do not know, they should go through the airport's official taxi stand where you can have at least some assurance that the driver is a known quantity — though this is still no guarantee and is not nearly as good as having a trusted driver sent from a hotel or mission organization you are working with. It is also a wonderful idea, where possible, to have your taxi fare negotiated and settled in advance at the airport taxi stand to ensure that you don't get taken for a ride literally and figuratively. Of course, like many things, there is a big difference in different locations and cultures. Travelers are far safer taking rides with unknown taxi drivers in Tokyo than they are Tegucigalpa.

Once again, when travelers are getting into a cab, they must pay close attention to their baggage. They should not set carry-on bags on the ground or on the taxi seat as they help load the larger luggage into the trunk of the cab or oversee the loading of this larger luggage. If they do, they may just look up to find that carry-on bag disappearing down the street in the hands of a very fast thief.

Sometimes airport employees can function as scouts for criminals waiting outside the airport, so it is not good to spend time waiting outside the airport exit doors. Get your luggage, get into your vehicle and clear the area as efficiently as possible.

There are often ATM machines in airport arrival halls, but it is far better to use an ATM machine or exchange bureau in the secure area of the airport if at all possible. If you must use the ATM machine in the arrival hall, pay close attention to people around you, watch your luggage carefully, and only take out the minimum amount needed to get to your hotel or mission center. Withdrawing a large amount of cash at an arrival hall ATM will often bring you to the attention of criminals.

Many times travelers also must pass through bus or train terminals, and these tend to be even more crime-ridden than airports. We will discuss security bus and train terminals in Chapter Seven, Security on the Street.

Air Safety

In many parts of the world, air travel can be dangerous because of lax maintenance and safety and security procedures. This is especially true in the developing world, where maintenance regulations and procedures often are not strictly enforced. The U.S. Federal Aviation Administration prohibits U.S. carriers from flying into foreign airports that do not meet security and safety standards. According to the FAA, at the time of this writing, 22 of the 94 foreign civil aviation authorities do not meet the standards of the FAA's International Aviation Safety Assessment program. The FAA's list of countries who do not meet these standards can be found here: http://www.faa.gov/passengers/international_travel/

In addition to the American FAA, the European Union provides a list of airlines it considers to be to unsafe to fly to or within the EU. That list can be found at: http://ec.europa.eu/transport/modes/air/safety/air-ban/index_en.htm

Additional data pertaining to airline safety can be found at the International Air Transit Association: http://www.iata.org/, the Flight Safety Foundation: http://flightsafety.org/ and websites such as http://planecrashinfo.com/ .

The consular information sheets previously discussed, and found at the http://travel.state.gov website, contain a section pertaining to aviation safety oversight in each specific country and will recommend against travel on unsafe airlines.

CHAPTER SIX:
SECURITY AT YOUR HOTEL
OR MISSION CENTER

Do not lurk like a thief near the house of the righteous, do not plunder their dwelling place;

— Proverbs 24:15

In this chapter we will discuss how to keep yourself and your gear safe while you are staying in a hotel or mission center. As with airports and aircraft, there are two basic threats we will discuss: criminals and terrorists. Again, you are more likely to be victimized by a criminal than a terrorist, but we will cover the terrorist threat for people who are going to be visiting more dangerous places. Obviously, some of the things we will talk about in this chapter regarding the terrorist threat will be less relevant to people going to lower-threat countries.

The Terrorist Threat

During the 1980s and 1990s there were a lot of attacks against embassies — not only the high-profile bombings of the U.S. embassies in places like Beirut, Lebanon and Nairobi, Kenya, but also incidents like the December 1996 seizure of the Japanese ambassador's residence in Lima, Peru. In response to this wave of attacks, the United States and many other countries have increased security at embassies and other diplomatic facilities. These facilities have been transformed into veritable fortresses and they are more difficult to attack than ever before. They have become what we refer to has "hard" targets due to the difficulty of successfully attacking them. These defensive measures caused a shift in terrorist targeting, and in the 2000s terrorists began focusing on softer symbols of Western influence, including hotels, resorts and restaurants.

A strike on an international hotel or resort can make almost the same kind of statement against the West as a strike on an embassy. Hotels are often full of Western business travelers, diplomats, intelligence officers and, not insignificantly, members of the media. This has made hotels target-rich environments for militants seeking to kill Westerners and gain international media attention without having to penetrate the extreme security of a hard target like a modern embassy.

Following the increase in hotel attacks worldwide, the larger chain hotels have implemented stricter security measures, hiring private security staff, erecting vehicle barriers and operating multi-layered checkpoints staffed by armed guards who use metal detectors to screen visitors.

When the shift toward attacking hotels instead of embassies began, the perpetrators usually relied on car or truck bombs that they could ram into a hotel lobby. As some hotels erected concrete barriers to counteract the threat from vehicle bombs, terrorists began using suicide bombers who could walk past security and into a crowded room, such as a restaurant or ballroom, before detonating their devices. Hotels responded by increasing the screening of pedestrians entering their premises.

In much the same way that the increase in embassy security shifted the threat toward hotels, the increase in hotel security has served to shift the threat to the housing compounds of non-governmental organizations, the United Nations and aid organizations, including Christian mission organizations.

Many of these housing compounds have also increased their security, but in most cases, these organizations simply do not have the resources to afford the same type of security afforded to major hotel chains or the United Nations. This often makes them more vulnerable targets than hotels.

In addition to security steps taken by the hotel or organization, there are things travelers can do to enhance their chances of avoiding or surviving a terrorist attack at their place of lodging. The first step is to learn whether adequate security measures are in place at the chosen location before making a reservation. Based upon the information about the threat environment in the country that was obtained while conducting the type of research discussed in Chapter Two, Before You Go, the traveler needs to determine if the security measures in place at the hotel or mission center are adequate to counter the threat.

Generally speaking, at a minimum, you are looking for a hotel with solid wood or metal doors that have deadbolts and peep holes. The secondary deadbolt locks are crucial, because hotel keys are easily copied and even modern electronic locks can be picked with electronic devices. If your hotel has a security chain or other type of additional lock, use it. A couple of twists on a security chain will take out some of the slack and make it more difficult to force open.

The rooms should also have sprinklers and smoke detectors and a phone that allows occupants to dial out. Also check the location and condition of fire extinguishers and hoses. It is also important to check emergency exits to ensure they are passable. When I was working on protective details overseas, I learned that it is not uncommon for emergency stairwells to be obstructed or even rendered impassible by items stored or stacked in them. It is also not unusual to find fire doors that have been chained shut due to the criminal threat.

Window locks and the locks on doors leading to adjoining rooms are also a concern and should be checked to make sure they work properly. If you can't lock all the doors and windows, ask for another room or move to another hotel.

Is the location of the hotel in a dangerous part of town, or one considered generally safe? Information about the neighborhood and the security measures in place at the facility is best acquired from a trusted associate or other source in the country, especially in the case of a hotel, because hotels have a financial incentive to provide hollow assurances. Reservation clerks will almost always assure you their establishment is safe. If you don't have a trusted contact in country, it might be worth a call to the regional security office at a U.S. embassy to see if they have an opinion about the hotel. It is important to keep in mind that the price of the hotel room is not always an indicator of the hotel's safety.

Once you are satisfied with the security at the location, the next step is to consider the security of the particular room you will stay in. In most hotels, some rooms are safer than others, and it is prudent to choose the safest room location possible. Generally, rooms above the second floor are safer than those on the ground floor, because a potential attacker cannot enter via the window or patio. However, due to the possibility of fire, you don't want to go more than five or six stories up so that you are not beyond the reach of a fire department rescue ladder.

Other rooms to avoid in high threat environments are those near the front of the hotel and those adjacent to the street. An attack against a hotel typically occurs in the foyer or lobby in the front of the building. In addition, in many countries, there is a threat of car bombs exploding on the street. Sometimes these are very powerful and can damage nearby buildings, so distance between your room and the street is a good thing. Do not be afraid to request another room if you believe the one the receptionist has assigned is not safe.

Finally, in high-threat environments it is best to avoid lingering in high-risk areas such as hotel lobbies, the front desk and entrance areas and restaurants. Western diplomats, business people and journalists who frequently congregate in these areas have been attacked on several occasions. In addition, unaccompanied luggage — which could contain a bomb — is most likely to be left near the front desk areas.

Should an attack occur, the best course of action is to avoid going to the primary attack zone. Travelers hearing shots or one explosion should avoid the temptation to run to their windows to see what happened. Instead, they should check their doors and take cover in a place away from the windows. Bathrooms with no windows are a good place to do this. Taking this step reduces the likelihood of being injured by a secondary explosion timed to kill survivors and first responders. In most large bombings, flying glass kills many of the victims. If no immediate danger from smoke or fire is present, unharmed guests should remain in their rooms and stay away from windows until rescue and security personnel arrive to secure the scene.

In the November 2008 hotel attacks in Mumbai, India, the attackers went room to room looking for Westerners. In several cases they were unable to open the doors and bypassed those rooms. Because of this, it is advisable to always lock and deadbolt your hotel doors. Travelers can also carry an inexpensive door wedge in their luggage. When properly used, a wedge can help your door from being forced open and provides extra security to help counter the problems with hotel door locks discussed above.

The Criminal Threat

A room above the second floor, but no higher than the sixth, is also generally safer from the criminal threat. If it is possible to climb from balcony to balcony, travelers should also keep their balcony doors and windows locked. Travelers also need to be very careful of rooms with security bars on the windows, because while they do provide some additional security from thieves, they can also make it difficult to get out of the room in case a fire blocks the hallway.

While in the hotel room, guests should avoid opening doors to unannounced visitors or those claiming to be delivering a package or conducting hotel maintenance. It is best in both cases to tell the caller to wait in the lobby and to check with the receptionist or hotel security. Most reputable hotels will not send a maintenance person to your room unannounced.

If your room has a safe, make sure it is securely bolted down and the bolts are not visible on the outside. If the bolts are exposed and are not welded, do not use the safe. An unsecured safe provides the thief a nice carrying case for your valuables and saves him the trouble of searching through your room. It is important to remember that these safes often have master keys that the hotel management keeps and they are not really all that secure. If you have valuable things that you do not wish to lose, either do not take them on the trip, or carry them with you. Do not leave them in your room unattended.

Practice good situational awareness, even while you are inside your hotel. If you sense that you are being followed or if a stranger is wandering the halls when you plan to enter your room, make your way to busy public areas instead (preferably the lobby) and notify hotel staff of the incident. Do not let a stranger follow you into your room. When you are in an elevator with other people, it is preferable to get on last and to be the last person to press the floor button. If someone around or in the elevator makes you uncomfortable, get out of it if you are in a public area of the hotel, or press a button that will take you to a public area of the hotel, such as the lobby or rooftop restaurant.

Just as in the airport, do not display your cash or other valuables at the hotel front desk, cashier or bar/restaurant. These are common places for criminals to lurk in wait for desirable targets.

If you are leaving your room, leave a light and the television on to give the impression that someone is in there. You can also hang the do not disturb sign on the door. Also, if you are leaving the hotel, it is a good idea to have a business card or slip of paper with the hotel name address and phone number on it. Keep this separate from your wallet in case you lose your wallet. This is especially important if you are in a country where you do not speak the language. You can use the card to show to a taxi driver so he knows where to take you.

Mission Centers

Depending on the country and the mission organization you are working with, you could be staying in a wide variety of accommodations ranging from very nice to fairly primitive conditions. This can include sleeping out of doors or in buildings with very little physical security. As discussed earlier, most mission organizations do not have the security budgets of Western hotel chains, so their security is generally not as good as hotels, and therefore many of the measures we discussed earlier regarding hotels do not apply to mission centers. As with a hotel, you will want to talk to the mission director or a friend who has stayed at the facility about the security of the mission center and the security situation in the area around it. This may or may not influence your decision to visit there, but it will definitely help in making decisions about what to take and what not to take on your mission trip. For example, if you are going to be staying in an area where crime or traffic make it too dangerous to walk or run for exercise, you might want to leave your workout gear at home.

One thing that can greatly help in the security of the mission facility is its relationship with the surrounding community. The neighbors will know who is supposed to be in the area and in some cases can warn mission organizations of suspicious behavior or actually take measures to encourage suspicious people to depart from the area.

Just as in a hotel, you want to pay attention to door and window locks. You also want to note if there are bars on the windows that would prevent you from using them as an exit in the event of a fire and plan accordingly. You should also note the location and condition of any fire extinguishers and fire hoses and check the fire escapes to make sure they are clear and unlocked.

Even though you are going to be staying in a compound with other Americans and with trusted local staff, you still need to guard your belongings. Do not tempt people by leaving valuables unattended. Remember that a smart phone is worth far more than many third-world workers make in an entire month. Also remember that passports are considered valuable. As previously mentioned, if possible, it is a good idea to gather up the passports of all the members of your group and lock them in a safe at the mission center. This not only protects them from theft, but also from loss. You will not be able to board the flight to go home if you misplace your passport, so securing them is very important. In most countries, you are fine to travel around the country with just a photocopy of your passport, but be sure to check the local regulations in the country you will be visiting. Some countries require foreign visitors to have their passports in their possession at all times.

Other Threats and Concerns

We've touched on fire a couple times in this chapter because fire is one of the most critical threats pertaining to lodging. In fact, fire kills far more people every year than terrorist attacks do. According to the World Health Organization, an estimated 195,000 people die each year from fire, while according to the Global Terrorism Database an average of 7,258 people die annually from terrorism, and that includes deaths in conflict zones such as Afghanistan and Iraq. Fire is a killer, and it does not threaten only wooden structures. A good illustration of the fire threat to concrete structures is the U.S. office building in Benghazi, Libya, which was attacked and burned on Sept. 11, 2012. As the video from news reports showed, the building was not structurally damaged during the attack.

What killed Ambassador Christopher Stevens and communications officer Sean Smith in Benghazi was not the fire, but the smoke and toxic fumes generated by the fire. Clearly, the danger of fire must be considered even in concrete buildings.

Statistics show that between 50 and 80 percent of all indoor fire fatalities are from smoke and fume inhalation. One way to protect yourself from smoke and fumes generated by a fire is to carry and use a smoke hood. As noted in the chapter on air travel, a smoke hood can be carried in a purse, backpack or briefcase and in many cases can provide you with enough clean air to escape from a burning building.

Just as in an aircraft, having a flashlight in case of a building fire can be very useful in helping you find your way out through the smoke. In any case, keeping a flashlight next to your bed will be helpful in case the electricity goes out — something that can be a daily occurrence in many parts of the world. It is also advisable to keep your hotel room key on the bedside table next to your flashlight.

Now, if you awake to the sound of a smoke alarm or to the smell of smoke in your room, get down on the floor and grab your hotel room key and flashlight. Don your smoke hood if you have one. Smoke and toxic gases tend to rise, so if you stand up you could end up directly in the smoke. At this point you should pause for just a moment to collect yourself and to assess your situation. Don't blindly panic and run out into the hallway — you could be running into trouble. Evacuate your room carefully and intentionally.

Before opening the door of your room, feel it with the palm of your hand. If the door or the doorknob is hot, there could be a fire in the hall right outside your room. Even if the door is not hot, open the door carefully and be prepared to slam it shut if there is fire in the hall.

If the hallway is clear of fire, crawl into the hallway. Staying low will keep you out of the smoke and toxic fumes. Closing the door behind you is a good idea, because it will help keep smoke out of your room in case you find the exit route obstructed and need to return to your room. Stay next to the wall to help guide you and to keep from being trampled by people who panic. Follow the hallway to the closest stairway fire exit and use them to get out. Never use an elevator during a fire. When you get to the exit stairs, walk down them to the ground floor. Holding onto the handrail will help guide you down the stairs and help prevent you from being knocked down and injured by panicking people.

If you encounter smoke in the stairwell, do not walk down into it. Also do not try to run through it, as the smoke and gasses may overcome you before you can get out of the building. Instead turn around and attempt to use another emergency exit. If there is also smoke coming up the second emergency staircase, you will have to decide whether to return to your room, or climb the stairs to the roof. If you do opt for the roof, prop the door open to allow the smoke to leave the stairwell and to prevent you from being locked out on the roof. You should try to find the part of the roof that is protected from fire and smoke and sit down.

If all your exits are blocked, or if there is fire in the hallway that prevents you from leaving your room, you should try to ventilate the smoke out of your room by turning on the bathroom fan and opening a window. You should avoid breaking the window unless you have to. Shards of glass can cut you or people below your window and you also might want to close the window if smoke begins to pour into your room through it.

If your room phone works, call the front desk or the fire department to tell them where you are in the building.

Hanging a bed sheet out of your window can also serve as a signal to firefighters.

If your water is still working, fill the bathtub with water to use in fighting the fire. You can use your ice bucket or trash-can to bail water onto your door or hot walls. You can also use the water to wet towels that you can push into the cracks around your door to help keep smoke out of your room. If you don't have a smoke hood, you can tie a wet towel around your head and over your nose and mouth to help reduce some of the smoke particles from getting into your lungs. But remember that this will not protect you from dangerous gases like carbon monoxide and hydrogen cyanide.

In many parts of the world, earthquakes also occasionally pose a serious threat. As illustrated by the January 2010 Haiti earthquakes, a severe seismic event can damage buildings. Indeed, most people killed in earthquakes die as a result of falling debris and not due to the movement of the earth itself. Because of this, it is best to get out of the building and into a clear area away from places where you can be struck by debris that can fall from buildings, or where electrical wires can fall. Unfortunately, though, is not always possible to get out of the building in time. If you are caught inside a building, seek shelter under a sturdy piece of furniture, like a dining room table.

Conventional wisdom is to seek shelter in a doorway during an earthquake, but doorways do not always provide true safety. Many interior doorways are not weight-bearing and do not provide any extra protection. Prior to an earthquake, you should examine the doorways of your hotel room or mission center room to ascertain if it is a sturdy weight-bearing doorway. Weight-bearing doorways are constructed in a manner that makes them sturdier than the walls around them, and they can provide some additional protection. Still, if you have the choice of getting out of the building or staying sheltered in a doorway, you should opt to get out of the building and into the open. If the earthquake is severe, you should get out of the building as soon as the shaking stops so that the building can be evaluated for structural damage and safety before you return.

If you are with a mission group, you should establish a rally point outside of your hotel or mission center that you can use in the case of a fire or earthquake, and clearly communicate to your team where the rally point is. The ability to account for the members of your team is crucial during a crisis.

Insects are another consideration related to lodging. In some tropical areas with heavy mosquito populations, the insects can carry diseases such as malaria and dengue fever. In such areas you might have to consider bringing a mosquito net for your bed if the mission center or hotel does not provide one. Travelers in some areas should also watch their shoes and other belongings for creepy crawlers such as scorpions and venomous spiders. A family friend found a couple of scorpions in her suitcase when she returned to the United States from Guatemala — fortunately she was not stung by either of them. Insects are another thing to ask about when talking to the mission organization or a friend who has been there in preparation for your trip. Having this information will also help you make informed decisions about things like whether to take malaria suppressants during your trip.

CHAPTER 7:
SECURITY ON THE STREET

Among my people are the wicked who lie in wait like men who snare birds and like those who set traps to catch people.

— Jeremiah 5:26

As mentioned in the last chapter, crime can affect travelers in their hotels or mission centers, but statistically, in most cities of the world, more people are victimized on the street than in their residences. While some people travel intending to stay inside an all-inclusive resort, most people travel to experience exciting and new things. In the case of short and long-term missions, we also travel to serve others as Christ's hands and feet. This means that we will not stay locked up in our mission centers or hotel rooms, but venture out into the streets where the people we want to serve are — and where there is more crime.

This is compounded by the fact that quite often the people we seek to reach and serve do not live in the best areas of town. Instead, they tend to live in slums, poor villages and sometimes even in dumps — places that normally have higher crime rates than exclusive neighborhoods.

Like airports, tourist attractions also tend to draw criminals due to the large number of potential victims they attract and the money and possessions those tourists tend to carry with them. It is very similar to the way a watering hole draws predators in the African savannah because of all the prey animals congregate there. The bottom line is that when we go out into the mission field or to a tourist site, we are exposing ourselves to more risk than if we had stayed inside our mission center or hotel. But, by taking a few simple steps, we can minimize the risk we are exposed to.

First, being alert and practicing good situational awareness is a must on the street, just as it is everywhere else. Yes, I know I am being repetitive, but there is a reason I devoted an entire chapter to situational awareness — it is the foundation for good personal security in any situation.

Second, something that goes hand-in-glove with situational awareness is common sense. Use your common sense to avoid dangerous areas and situations to the best of your ability. If something appears risky, don't do it — especially if it is not absolutely essential to your mission. Many times you can avoid problems simply by being agile and flexible. (This is something many Americans struggle with.) If a street gang does not want you to set up your medical clinic on a particular block, but you can set the clinic up a few blocks away and still provide care for the people you want to reach, be flexible and adjust your plans rather than provoke a confrontation with the gang over a non-essential principle. Many times Americans tend to cling to the concept that the rights and freedoms they enjoy in the United States should apply overseas, but that clearly is not the case. You need to understand the reality of how things work on the street in the culture where you are operating.

Now, that said, even going into a crime-ridden third world slum generally can be much safer if you go during daylight hours and work with local pastors and community leaders who know the lay of the land and can navigate you past potential problems. Heed the advice of such partners and do not be the pushy American.

Third, there is safety in numbers. When you are out on the street, the members of your mission team should always employ the buddy system and never, ever wander off alone. This is not an absolute guarantee of safety — in some places even large groups of tourists or missionaries can be the target of several well-armed men, but this does not happen that frequently, and most often it is the straggler who is targeted by criminals. This principle is especially true for women, who can be groped, sexually assaulted or even raped if caught alone and away from the group, but is equally applicable to men. When I was in Guatemala, we had a homicide case where two small Guatemalan men easily took care of a very large American man with the aid of their pistol. Even big guys need to use common sense and avoid traveling alone.

One of the things that will assist your efforts to be alert and practice common sense is to do some research on crime in the area you will be visiting in advance. It is dangerous to rely on assumptions. Every country and region can have different threats and criminal tactics, and understanding what those threats and criminal tactics are can guide what you are looking for when you are practicing good situational awareness to your surroundings. If you know travelers are frequently robbed on a particular stretch of road, and most frequently after dark, you can ensure that you only travel that road during daylight hours and increase your awareness as you travel that section of road. Sources that can provide information on crime in specific countries and cities include the consular information sheets and the OSAC crime and safety reports discussed in Chapter 2. In-country contacts and ministry partners can also provide useful information pertaining to local crime trends and tactics.

As previously mentioned, when you are on the street it is important not to draw attention to yourself. This includes not flashing your cash or jewelry and dressing modestly. If possible you should avoid looking like a tourist as much as possible, though sometimes this is difficult. My blonde wife, kids and I always stuck out as gringos when we lived in Guatemala and we still do when we work in Haitian villages in the Dominican Republic during our annual mission trip. But, by behaving and dressing in a culturally respectful manner and not drawing additional attention to ourselves, we attempt to mitigate this attention to the best of our ability. We have all seen obnoxious, obvious American tourists (and sadly, missionaries) — don't be one of those people.

Also, as previously discussed, by paying attention to your surroundings and not acting dazed and confused you can reduce your chance of being victimized by criminals. They also like to select targets that are distracted or impaired by substances like alcohol. Indeed, many of the assaults and homicides we investigated in Guatemala involved alcohol. But alcohol is not the only thing that can make us vulnerable on the street. People who are "tuned out" while listening to music, playing video games or who are involved in a telephone conversation can also become quite unaware of what is happening around them.

I want to repeat here what I noted in Chapter 3. I do not want you to be paranoid or looking for a criminal behind every bush as you are conducting ministry or visiting a tourist site. That not only kills your enjoyment, but also impairs your effectiveness in ministry. I urge you to be engaged with people and to show them Christ's love. But, at the same time, you need to practice the relaxed awareness we discussed. This not only allows you to notice people who are demonstrating a demeanor indicating they are hostile, or perhaps are casing you for a potential crime, but this awareness also opens your eyes to ministry opportunities. Paying attention helps you notice that very sad looking young girl who is separated from the crowd and is leaning against the tree instead of participating in the fun vacation Bible school games and lessons with the rest of the kids.

One other thing you should do as you are traveling about is to consciously identify places that can serve as safe havens. These are places you can run to in case you are confronted by a criminal and need help. These are normally places where there is a heightened security presence like a police station, military post, government building or a bank. In a third-world village or slum where such things are rare, they could also include places like a church or medical clinic where your group is conducting ministry and there is a large crowd of friendly people. Consciously identifying such places as you go will then allow you to quickly head for the closest safe location without having to think about it in case of a problem or emergency. Chances are that you will never need to head to a safe haven, but in that isolated instance where you would need to, it is good to be able to react without having to take time to think.

As mentioned in Chapter 4, it is also a very good idea to break up your cash into separate bundles and to keep your spending money separate from your larger bills. In addition to criminals who will confront you and rob you by threat of force, there are also criminals who will seek to steal by stealth.

This type of criminal includes pickpockets, snatch-and-grab artists, or diversion artists who will use some sort of distraction to divert your attention while they steal your belongings.

Pickpockets frequently work in tight crowds, which allow them to blend in and quickly disappear after their theft. They also like such locations because other people are jostling the victim, and that jostling allows them to pick pockets or purses and backpacks without being noticed. Pickpockets love wallets kept in men's back pockets or jacket/coat pockets. They also like to snatch women's wallets out of open purses.

Common distraction robberies can involve things like spilling food or a drink on your clothing and pickpocketing you while wiping it off, asking you to look at a map or brochure, or someone splashing mud or muddy water on your clothing. There are several other common street scams that involve someone dropping a wallet or wad of bills for you to pick up, or someone approaching you with a wallet or wad of bills before an accomplice approaches, pretending to be a policeman or the owner of the wallet or money.

The creativity of some criminals is really quite amazing, and the types of schemes they create to steal from people are nearly limitless. It is also important to remember that many pickpockets work as teams, so beware of the old lady conveniently coming up to you with the damp rag after the young man squirts ketchup on you.

Another scam involves having a child come up to you and pester you and then when a parent intervenes to help you, the child picks your pockets while you are distracted. Just because a child is involved does not mean the incident is innocuous. In some parts of the world there are wolf packs of street kids who will swarm and steal things from people. Even though you are much larger than the children, when they swarm you it is almost impossible to protect your belongings from all those sets of little hands. The kids who get the goods will then race away while the others hamper your pursuit.

When I lived in Guatemala City, there were groups of young homeless kids who would emerge after dark and roam the streets of the city's center. They abused inhalants like rubber cement or gasoline, and many of them suffered brain damage from sustained inhalant use to the point where they could not talk intelligibly. Since I am a dad, these kids broke my heart, but I always sought to avoid them by reminding myself of the threat they posed and I never took my eyes off of them. A friend of mine was not so lucky. She was mugged in Buenos Aires when she allowed a small street kid to get close enough behind her to stick a knife against her back. She had figured the kid was so small that he did not pose a real threat, but his knife changed that perception very quickly. Once the first kid got the drop on her, his friends quickly swarmed her and they relieved her of her purse and cell phone. Fortunately, that is all they did to her.

A friend has told me of an incident he experienced in Moscow's Red Square in which a pack of street children mobbed a pastor who was a member of a short-term mission trip my friend was guiding. As the pastor was being "hugged," he yelled over to the rest of the group "Hey, look these kids love me!" As my friend yelled out a warning, the kids scattered and the pastor noticed he had been relieved of his camera. Fortunately, in this case, the group yelled and alerted the Moscow police officers stationed on the square who were able to recover the camera from the children.

Snatch-and-grab artists sometime work on foot, and those on foot will run after slicing through a purse strap or grabbing a chain, camera, cell phone, earring or pair of sunglasses. Other snatchers will work on bicycles, motorbikes or even in cars. They possess the hand-eye coordination to precisely snatch something from your body while moving. These mobile criminals pose a danger in that sometimes they will not be able to cleanly cut the purse strap and can sometimes drag a victim for some distance if they are operating in a car. If you are caught in that situation, it is better to let your purse go than to allow yourself to be dragged and badly injured. They can also sometimes slice victims accidentally with their knives or razors.

Backpacks, fanny packs, shopping bags, suitcases, cameras and briefcases can be snatched in a similar fashion. Thieves often hone in on things like purses and backpacks because they perceive — usually correctly — that they hold items of value. Because of this you need to always be careful when carrying one on the street, and you should avoid carrying them altogether if it is possible. If you do need to carry some sort of bag to tote items such as sunscreen, insect repellent, hand sanitizer or drinking water, you should avoid putting your valuables inside the bag too. It is a lot less painful to see your bag of sunscreen and water disappearing down the street in the hands of a criminal than it is a bag with your wallet and cell phone.

Besides, if you have minimized your possessions as we discussed in Chapter 4, you shouldn't need a bag to carry your valuables. A number of vendors sell pouches and travel garments with extra interior pockets that can help protect your items from pickpockets and bag snatchers if you have more things than you can carry in your two front pockets.

Other criminals will use a razorblade to slit open a purse, backpack or other bag and steal the contents. Like pickpocketing, this happens most frequently in a crowded location, and while it most often happens to stationary targets it can also be done to someone walking. Because of this, if you are traveling with a bag or purse, it is better to have it clasped in front of you than on your shoulder or back. But even that is no guarantee someone will not attempt to snatch your bag.

It is important to remember that even these types of criminals — pickpockets and snatch artists — do casing, or preoperational surveillance, before they attempt their crime, and they are vulnerable to detection during that period of time. This type of criminal normally does not like confrontation and prefers to prey on non-suspecting victims. By noticing such a criminal in the surveillance stage, you can usually cause them to divert to a less alert target and avoid being a victim. I have personally experienced this principle many times in a number of different countries when I have made potential criminals very uncomfortable by simply paying attention to them.

Automatic Teller Machines

In Chapter 5 we discussed using the ATM at the airport and noted how you should attempt to use an ATM on the secured side of the airport rather than on the non-secured side. Outside of the airport, the best locations for ATM use are also in more secure locations such as inside a bank or in a hotel lobby. I say "more secure" because criminals will sometimes set up in busy hotel lobbies to look for victims. Many hotel cashiers abroad will also process cash advances from the traveler's credit card account or exchange U.S. dollars into local currencies. As previously mentioned, traveler's checks also can reduce dependence on ATMs altogether if they are accepted in your destination country.

One key to avoid using ATMs at risky times or in risky locations is to plan ahead and have the correct amount of cash needed for the day's or night's activities. This way you can choose a good ATM location rather than finding yourself in a bind where you are forced to use a poorly lit ATM on the street at night in order to get enough cash to catch a taxi back to your hotel or mission center.

When using an ATM, it is important to pay attention to the people and the environment around the ATM location and not focus on the machine itself. This lack of situational awareness leads to people being victimized by ambush-type criminals lurking in the area. This can result in robbery or, even worse, to an "express" kidnapping, in which the victim is abducted and forced to withdraw money from his or her bank account from an ATM until the balance in the account connected to the card is exhausted. Kidnappers who discover there is a large balance in the account linked to their victim's ATM card have been known to hold on to the traveler until the account is depleted. Some victims have spent days stuffed in the trunk of a car during protracted express kidnappings.

To minimize this danger, many travelers choose to travel with a prepaid bank card — usually obtained at one's local bank — that has a limited amount of money in the account or they travel with an ATM card that is just connected to their checking account rather than their larger savings bank account.

Another type of crime connected to ATMs is "skimming." This crime involves placing a device that looks like part of the machine over the ATM's card slot. The device contains a card reader that records account information when the victim attempts to use the ATM machine, allowing cyber-criminals access to bank account information. In many cases a camera also is placed on the machine to record PIN numbers. Armed with a victim's card and PIN numbers, the skimmers can then create a clone of the victim's ATM card and deplete his account. Some ATMs also have doors that require the bank customer to swipe an ATM card to enter. Criminals have also placed skimmers on these card slots.

Skimmers come in a wide variety of shapes and sizes. You can see what some of them look like by doing a Google image search for "ATM skimmers." Skimmers are far more common at out-of-the-way ATMs where criminals have the opportunity to place them without being seen than they are in ATMs in heavily traveled places such as inside banks or hotel lobbies. Nonetheless, you should look for signs of skimmers even on these ATM machines.

Another security concern related to money on the street is the currency exchange rate. The exchange rate is obviously important if you want to understand the value of items you wish to buy in the local currency, but there are some other important implications. First, the official exchange rate in some countries can vary dramatically from the unofficial, or black-market, rate on the street. This happens often in tightly controlled economies and is almost always artificially skewed in the host country's favor. Quite often drug dealers and other criminals will also offer a generous rate as they attempt to launder the proceeds from their illegal activities. They are willing to lose a few percentage points of value to get their money cleaned.

The opportunity to obtain more local currency for their dollars often tempts travelers to take part in informal currency exchanges on the street or even in established places of business that are unauthorized to change cash. But, travelers who participate in such illegal practices put themselves at risk of being deported or even jailed in some cases. This practice also opens up the possibility of receiving counterfeit money — counterfeiters also offer generous exchange rates — which further puts the traveler at risk of ending up on the wrong side of the law. As Christians we are clearly called to "render unto Caesar" and to be above reproach. This applies even in instances where the host country government is playing games with the value of their currency, and Christians should not engage in the black market for monetary gain.

Another drawback of exchanging money on the black market is that it also puts you in close proximity with the local criminal element, which is often synonymous with organized crime. What starts out as an informal money exchange can easily end up becoming a robbery or kidnapping. Generally speaking, if the exchange rate offered by someone on the street sounds too good to be true, it probably is.

Like black market currency, another thing that can get people into trouble is antiquities. As mentioned in Chapter 2, be very careful in regard to cultural artifacts and antiquities — either those you purchase or those given as a gift. The person giving you a gift might not know what the value of the item is, and you could find yourself in trouble with the local government authorities or with U.S. Customs authorities upon your return to the United States.

As previously mentioned, it is very important to know and observe local norms and customs. In terms of ministry this really matters, because offending the people you are attempting to minister to is quite counterproductive. But there are also security implications. Don't offend a tribal elder or other person by flatly refusing a gift, but check with your contact with the local mission organization you are working with before attempting to take such a gift out of the country.

And speaking of culture, in many cultures, women dress more conservatively than they do in the United States. This is a simple fact. If American women traveling to such places do not respect the local dress codes, not only will they have a chance of offending people, but also they will frequently be thought of as being immodest or considered as prostitutes, and this can draw unwanted sexual attention.

Another cultural difference that many people encounter when they travel overseas are protests that can be more frequent and more violent than those in the United States. The reasons for such demonstrations can range from labor disputes to political problems to outrage over incidents such as the cartoons of the Prophet Mohammed. Obviously, American travelers should avoid anti-American and anti-European protests, as they could come to the attention of the angry protesters and be attacked. But even if the protesters' focus is something else, like the local government, you should do your best to avoid the area of the protest.

In many countries, the police are quite free in their use of rubber bullets and tear gas, and the protesters can be equally prolific in their hurling of stones and Molotov cocktails. You do not want to get caught in the middle of such a melee. In recent years, American travelers have been injured in Arab Spring protests in places like Egypt. Some protesters have also sexually assaulted foreign females.

In addition to government buildings and foreign embassies, Western restaurants and hotels are common targets for attacks by mobs of protesters. Since these mobs often light such places on fire, it is best to avoid them during a protest.

A hotel, restaurant or bank may have relatively good physical security measures, such as concrete barriers, and hardened doors and windows, but while these can help protect a facility against a terrorist attack they can do little to prevent an angry mob from overrunning a property. Protesters can scale barriers, and their overwhelming numbers can render most security measures useless. The recently released movie *Argo* provided a good depiction of how that worked when the U.S. Embassy in Tehran was overrun by an angry mob in 1979, and the September 2012 attack on the U.S. Embassy in Tunis demonstrates the awesome destructive power of large crowds.

If protesters set fire to the building, as happened at the U.S. Embassy in Islamabad in 1979 (same year as Tehran), even an armored safe room can become a death trap. Indeed, once a mob attacks, there often is little that can be done. At that point, the focus should be on preventing injuries and saving lives.

When a protest spirals into violence, the only real choice for most people is to escape the area and wait for the violence to subside. This obviously works best when the protest is confined to one area — as opposed to a major citywide riot. It obviously is best if you know of such protests in advance and can stay away from the area where they are until they are over. Once you know of a protest, you should try to track it through media and other reports so that you can activate contingency plans if the angry mob begins to move toward your location.

Public Transportation

Like airports, taxi stands and bus and train terminals are spots that tend to attract criminals. Because of this you should always stay alert for pickpockets and other petty thieves in such places.

Bus and subway platforms are prime areas for the type of jostling action we previously discussed in regard to pickpockets. Unfortunately, in many countries this does not stop once you get on the train or bus. Passengers are often packed into such conveyances like sardines, and this gives a thief a very good opportunity to pick your pocket or slit your bag. It is also not unusual for women to be groped or sexually assaulted on packed trains and buses. This is not just a third-world issue; in Tokyo, where the subways are very crowded, they have special women-only cars on subways due to the high incidence of sexual assaults. One way to avoid this subway craziness is to take the train at off-peak hours rather than during the heart of the morning and afternoon rush hours (and these times may vary from city to city, so check on them). It is also better to take a subway car in the middle of the train rather than the last car, and to use a car with other passengers in it.

When I lived in Guatemala, old U.S. school buses served as cheap inner city and inter-city transportation. We called them chicken buses, because quite often you would see people on them holding chickens on their laps. In order to maximize their profits, the drivers and conductors of these buses would jam as many people as possible into the seats. Quite frequently they would try to squeeze three people into a seat meant to fit two U.S. schoolchildren, then continue to jam more people in, either sitting on suitcases or standing in the aisle. A large number of Peace Corps volunteers and other Americans were robbed of their wallets and passports while traveling in chicken buses — frequently by people slitting their backpacks. These buses are also safety hazards, being old and poorly maintained, so I recommend avoiding such transportation wherever possible.

In some cities, the bus systems are fine to use. If you are taking the bus, it is better to sit up front near the driver and on the aisle. For inter-city travel it is far safer to pay a little bit extra in order to take a nicer bus with assigned seating. You should also attempt to take as little luggage with you as possible — ideally no more than you can comfortably carry.

Taxis can be very convenient, but as noted in Chapter 5, they can also be dangerous. The same rules apply to taking a taxi on the street as taking a taxi from the airport. Only use an official taxi, often called a radio taxi, instead of an unlicensed taxi, even though unlicensed taxis may offer discounted rates. In many countries taxi drivers will steal from customers by taking them on unnecessarily long rides, and they can sometimes also set customers up for a robbery or kidnaping. It is obviously good to check a map before your trip and know the distance your trip should be before leaving your hotel or mission center. Normally the hotel doorman will ensure you get a reliable taxi at your hotel, and you can often get the number for the company the hotel uses from the doorman so you can call for a cab when you need to return to your hotel. You can also get the phone number for a reputable taxi company from your local ministry contact, and in many countries restaurant doormen will also steer you toward reputable taxis.

If you are going to be traveling by taxi in a country where you don't speak the language, have the address of your various destinations written out in the local language and carry it with you so you can show the driver.

The buddy rule also applies in public transportation. Try not to travel alone in a taxi, bus or train. If possible, try to minimize your travel at night. If you must travel at night, use stations that are busy and well-lit.

Walking is quite safe in many countries, but is dangerous in others due to crime or because of the lack of sidewalks and abundance of crazy drivers. This is another thing to research before your trip and to check with your local ministry partners before doing.

CHAPTER 8:
WHEN THINGS GO BAD

I look for help, O Sovereign Lord. You are my refuge; don't let them kill me. Keep me from the traps they have sent for me, from the snares of those who do wrong.

— Psalm 141:8-9

While God will protect us from many dangers, there are times when His plans, or our mistakes, cause us to face bad situations. Sometimes, like Paul and Silas in Philippi, God will pull us through these situations without serious long-term harm. Other times, like when Paul was beheaded by the Emperor Nero, these situations can prove to be fatal.

There are cases when God will allow us to understand what He is trying to accomplish through tragedy. Following the deaths of five missionaries in Ecuador in January 1956, the families and coworkers of those five men were able to see a rapid and dramatic breakthrough as the Waorani people responded to the Gospel. But events do not always transpire in such a storybook fashion. There are times when we simply don't have the opportunity to see and understand how God uses bad situations to work for his glory. As Isaiah 55:8-9 remind us, God is transcendent and His ways are not our ways.

Over the past few chapters we have discussed practicing good security at airports, while in hotels or mission centers, while on the street and while taking public transportation. Unfortunately, the world is a dangerous place filled with sinful people, and even people who practice good situational awareness and good personal security can sometimes find themselves either confronted by an armed assailant or actually coming under fire in an active shooter scenario. Because of this, I thought it might be useful to discuss such situations and how to react when caught in one.

Mindset

Perhaps the most important factor affecting a person's reaction to a life-threatening incident is their mindset going into the situation. As we noted in Chapter 3 when discussing situational awareness, the way our brains are engineered makes it very difficult for a person to go from a state of being "tuned out" and completely unaware of what is going on around them to a state of high alert. When confronted by such a jump, it is not uncommon for people to freeze, go into shock and become totally unable to respond to the situation confronting them. This type of panic-induced paralysis can be extremely deadly, and at that point the only hope of surviving an incident is sheer luck or divine providence. People in such a state can do nothing to save themselves.

Another factor of this mindset is the need for people to recognize that there are bad people in the world who want to hurt innocent people, and that they could be potential targets.

This means that people must not only practice situational awareness but also trust their guts when they feel something isn't quite right. Denial can be a very dangerous thing when it overrides or rationalizes away gut feelings of danger. Over my former careers as a special agent and corporate security officer, I have interviewed numerous people who allowed denial to override suspicious indicators they noted, and who then proceeded to do things that resulted in their victimization — all because they had the mindset that they could not possibly become victims. In shooting situations, I have spoken with victims who did not realize that shots were actually being fired and instead dismissed them as pranks or fireworks. I have seen media reports of similar remarks from witnesses regarding recent shooting incidents, such as the July 20, 2012, shooting at a movie theater in Aurora, Colorado. In short, denial is deadly.

By practicing the proper level of situational awareness and understanding the possibility of being targeted, a person will be mentally prepared to realize that an attack is happening — something security professionals refer to as attack recognition. The earlier a target recognizes he or she is under attack, the better. When a criminal is planning an attack — even an ambush criminal like a purse-snatcher or a rapist — he has already selected an area in which to conduct the attack, or an attack zone. Once the victim gets to the attack zone — driving into a specific intersection in the case of a kidnapping, or perhaps coming within arm's length of a purse-snatcher — the criminal will then launch the attack. But if a potential victim sees the criminal, realizes he or she is approaching an attack zone and recognizes that an attack is coming, many times they can stop, turn around and avoid the problem before the trap can be sprung and the criminal attack launched. You can run away before the kidnappers block your car in, before a mugger grabs you or has the chance to fully pull his gun out of his pocket.

Most often, when a criminal loses the element of surprise he will not follow a victim who departs from the attack zone and darts to a safe place. Even once the attack begins to unfold, often the victim can still keep it from being successful by quickly recognizing it and getting out of the attack zone.

Remember, criminal attacks do not appear out of a vacuum. They are the result of a planning process that can be recognized if one is looking for it. As noted in Chapter 3, criminals tend to be very bad at camouflaging their actions, and their suspicious demeanor often leaves them vulnerable to early detection.

Now, admittedly, there is the slight danger of embarrassment in the aftermath of a false reaction. I have blushed after taking cover in response to unexpected celebratory gunfire by wedding guests when I was walking down the street in Yemen, but in general it is far better to initially overreact and be a little embarrassed when there is no threat than it is to underreact in a truly dangerous situation.

While it is obviously best to avoid danger and leave an area before a crime is launched or weapons used, this cannot always be accomplished. Some attacks simply cannot be avoided. But that said, even if you cannot avoid an attack, recognizing danger immediately and then quickly taking action to attempt to mitigate the threat can often mean the difference between survival and death.

Compliance or Resistance?

If you are caught in a situation in which you cannot avoid an attack and an armed criminal confronts you, you must then choose your course of action. Quickly processing the events that are unfolding and analyzing the criminal's intent will make a huge difference in which action you choose.

Generally speaking, you have two essential choices. You can comply with the criminal's demands, or you can resist by fighting or fleeing. In many situations, the criminal does not want to hurt you — he merely wants to steal something you have. In such a case, the choice is easy — give up the goods. It is simply not worth being injured or killed over some money or your watch. Generally, criminals in the third world are not concerned about being caught by the police, so they have no reason to kill you to prevent you from identifying them. They simply want to relieve you of your belongings and move on. However, life is quite cheap in the third world, and in many places criminals will not hesitate to use gratuitous violence or to kill you if you do not give them what they demand.

But this is where research is a critical factor. You need to know the tendencies of the criminals in the area where you are going to be traveling. Do they threaten but then not use force against victims who comply? Do they generally shoot first and then take what they want off the bodies? Do they kidnap victims instead of just robbing them? Do they tend to sexually assault female victims? The answers to these questions will help you place what is happening to you in the proper context so that you can conduct a quick assessment and determine what to do next.

In general, I would suggest complying with a criminal when death or severe physical harm is not imminent and the criminal is using his weapon only to threaten you in order to take something that is not worth your life. (However, this can change very quickly, and you need to keep a very close eye on the criminal in order to assess the state of his mind and any signs that his intent is changing.)

You should attempt to resist or escape when the criminal does not yet have you under control and a viable escape route exists. You should also resist or escape when the criminal has already begun attempting to cause you serious harm, or you sense the criminal is about to take some action that could cause you serious injury or death.

You have a hard decision to make if the criminal tries to take you from the initial attack site to a secondary crime scene. Crime statistics show clearly that when a victim is moved from the place of the original encounter to a second location, the secondary crime scene, his or her chance of being seriously injured or killed increases dramatically. Most predatory criminals like rapists or serial killers will take their victims to a place where they feel safer and where they can control the victim.

The same is true for kidnapping gangs; once they take you from the place of abduction to the place where they plan to hold you (often called the safe house), your chance of escape is reduced greatly. At the safe house, the criminals ordinarily have means to restrain their victims, such as cages or shackles, and they will often have designated guards to watch you. Therefore, the best time to escape from a kidnapping gang is at the initial abduction site.

Let's now talk a little more about resistance and escape.

Run, Hide, Fight

Some people have been critical of the simplicity of the "Run, Hide, Fight" public service video that was produced by the City of Houston and funded by the U.S. Department of Homeland Security when the video was made available to the public on YouTube. But in my assessment, the video does a pretty good job of achieving its goal of raising awareness of active shooter situations and of providing a simple, easy-to-remember mantra similar to the "stop, drop and roll" fire-prevention slogan. The video also discusses the necessity of having an evacuation plan and being aware of surroundings. Is the video a complete self-defense course? Clearly not, but it does meet its limited objectives.

Once people have recognized that an attack is taking place, a critical step must be taken before they can decide to run, hide or fight: They must determine where the gunfire (or threat) is coming from. Without doing so, victims could run blindly from a position of relative safety into danger. I certainly encourage anyone under attack to get out of the attack site and run away from danger, but you must first ascertain that you are in the attack site before taking action.

Many times, the source of the threat will be evident and will not take much time to locate. But sometimes, depending on the location — whether in a building or out on the street — the sounds of gunfire can echo and it may take a few seconds to determine the direction it is coming from. In such a scenario, it is prudent to quickly take cover until the source and direction of the threat can be located. As you take cover, you may learn that the gunfire is benign, as I did in Yemen. In other instances you will learn there is indeed a gunman posing a threat, and in some instances there could be more than one gunman, which could complicate escape plans.

Fortunately, most attackers engaging in active shooter scenarios are not well-trained. They tend to be poor marksmen who lack tactical experience with their weapons. For example, in his attack on a Los Angeles Jewish community center daycare on Aug. 10, 1999, Buford Furrow fired 70 shots from an Uzi-style submachine gun but only wounded five people. The Uzi is an effective and highly accurate weapon at short distances, which means the only reason Furrow did so little damage was his poor marksmanship. During the July 20, 2012, shooting in Aurora, Colorado, James Holmes only managed to kill 12 people — despite achieving almost total tactical surprise in a fully packed theater. This was due to a combination of poor marksmanship and his inability to clear a malfunction from his rifle.

This typical lack of marksmanship implies that most people killed in active shooter situations are shot at very close range. There are some obvious exceptions, like the shooting at the University of Texas on Aug. 1, 1966, when ex-Marine Charles Whitman shot several people from the top of a tower on the college campus. But even then, most of Whitman's victims were shot early on in his attack, and his ability to successfully engage targets declined rapidly as victims realized where the shots were coming from and either moved away from the threat or took cover and waited for the authorities to respond.

MDACC

As in the U.T. Tower case, potential victims can do several things to reduce their chances of being shot, even when confronted by a trained shooter. We use an old acronym to describe these steps: MDACC, which stands for motion, distance, angle, cover and concealment.

First, it is much harder to shoot a moving target than a stationary one, especially if that target is moving at a distance. Most tactical shootings happen at distances of less than 7 meters. Indeed, there are very few people who can consistently hit a stationary target beyond 25 meters with a pistol, much less a moving target. Most people can put 25 meters between them and an attacker in just a few seconds, so motion and distance are your friends.

The angle between the target and the shooter is also important, because shooting a target running away in a straight line is easier than shooting a target running away at an angle, since the second scenario requires the shooter to swing the barrel of the weapon and lead the target. Both require a good deal of practice, even with a rifle or shotgun. If the target can run at an angle behind objects like trees, cars, office furniture or walls that obstruct the shooter's view of the target (concealment) or stop bullets (cover), that is even more effective.

Whether running or trying to hide, it is important to distinguish between concealment and cover. Items that provide concealment will hide you from the shooter's eye but will not protect you from bullets. A bush or tree leaves may provide concealment, but only a substantial tree trunk will provide cover. A typical office drywall-construction interior wall will provide concealment but not cover. This means that if a person is forced to hide inside an office or hotel, they might be able to lock the door but the shooter will in all likelihood still be able to fire through the walls and the door. Still, if the shooter cannot see his or her target, he will be firing by chance rather than intentionally aiming, and the chance of hitting the target is therefore greatly reduced.

In any case, those hiding inside a room should attempt to find some sort of additional cover, like a bed, dresser or heavy desk. It is always better to find cover than concealment, but even partial cover — something that will only deflect or fragment the projectiles — is better than no cover at all.

Even if you determine that you are not the target of the gunman — the gunfire is the result of a confrontation between criminal groups, or a criminal and the police, for example — you should still seek cover because there is still a chance of being hit by a stray bullet. Resist the urge to see the excitement and keep your head down and behind cover.

Fight

Sometimes you could be in a situation where you face imminent harm and you do not have an opportunity to run. When someone is already shooting or about to shoot, most people freeze, but this is the time when you must fight. How you fight will obviously be dictated by your experience and training, but if you decide to fight, it is best not to telegraph your intentions. You can talk like you are going to comply while acting quickly and savagely.

If you have received some high-quality self-defense training, you know that if you can get a shooter to come within arm's length, you can at least momentarily get yourself out of the line of fire by acting quickly. Action is always faster than reaction, and if you move quickly enough without telegraphing your motion, you can position your body to the side of and behind the muzzle of the gun before even the most alert shooter can pull the trigger. Raising your hands in a move of apparent surrender and verbalization can serve as helpful distractions as well.

What happens next depends on your training. You can control the gun and disarm the criminal (easier than it sounds if you have been taught how) or simply use all the force you have to push the shooter off balance, so you can make a break for it and begin to employ the principles of MDACC to escape.

If you find yourself caught in a struggle with a criminal, use whatever weapons you have at hand (including the criminal's) and do whatever you can to incapacitate the criminal so that you can escape. When you are fighting for your life, there is no such thing as a dirty fight. You must unleash your inner warrior and fight to defend your life or the lives of those you are protecting.

Again, resisting is risky, but if you are caught in a situation where you have no viable choice, you must resist, and while you are resisting — or escaping for that matter — you could be wounded.

Wounds and the Inner Warrior

Like almost everything we discuss in this chapter, mindset is critical when a person is wounded. In shooting situations it is not unusual for many more people to be wounded than killed. This is often related to the issue of poor marksmanship discussed above. In such a situation, it is extremely important for the wounded person to understand that, unlike what you see in the movies, most gunshot wounds are not immediately fatal and rarely immobilize the victim right away. However, it is not uncommon for people to drop to the ground when they are shot and freeze in panic or go into shock. This gives the shooter an opportunity to approach them for a point-blank coup de grace.

It is very important for people to realize that most gunshots are survivable and that, even after being wounded, their bodies can continue to function to get them away from the attack site and to safety. Certainly, once a target gets out of the immediate danger zone they will want to seek first aid or treat themselves with improvised pressure bandages to stop the bleeding and avoid going into shock. Modern trauma medicine is very good, and as seen in the Aurora, Colorado, shooting mentioned above, most victims wounded in these types of attacks will survive if they get prompt medical assistance.

It is no mistake that training regimens for special operations forces soldiers and competitive athletes place so much emphasis on the mental aspect of combat and sports — that is, learning that your body can keep functioning and continue to do amazing things, even after your mind has told you that it is time to quit. That same sense of drive and determination, the inner warrior, can help keep a person's body functioning after they have been wounded.

The inner warrior is also critical in keeping you going after you have been robbed or assaulted. But as Christians we have another important source of strength: the power of the Holy Spirit working in us to guide us, protect us and strengthen us.

Scripture tells us a lot of things about David. It tells us that he was a musician, a poet and a king. He was also a formidable warrior who not only slew the giant Goliath, but also hundreds of other men. Saul demanded the foreskins of 100 Philistines before he would allow David to marry his daughter Michal, and David brought him 200. Yet despite David's strength, skill and bravery, he did not rely on his own abilities. He constantly sought God's help to protect, strengthen and guide him. We know this from reading the Psalms that David wrote in which he frequently asked God for these specific things, like in Psalm 141, which I quoted at the beginning of this chapter.

I believe that we also need to pray to God for these same things as we go into the mission field. In addition to surrendering our wills and praying for opportunities to be God's hands and feet, we should also ask for Him to guide our steps and provide us with the situational awareness that will allow us to avoid the traps and snares of evil men and to pass by in safety. As we close this book, it is my prayer that our God will guide you and protect you.

ABOUT THE AUTHOR

Scott Stewart is the vice president of analysis at Stratfor, a global intelligence company. He is a former Diplomatic Security Service (DSS) special agent who investigated hundreds of terrorism cases, spanning the globe from Albania to Yemen. Most notably, he was the lead State Department investigator of the 1993 World Trade Center bombing and the follow-on investigation of the thwarted "N.Y. Bomb Plot."

Scott also served as a member of the U.S. government's Interagency Hostage Location Task Force and was part of the American team that debriefed Anglican envoy Terry Waite upon his release from captivity in Lebanon in 1991.

From 1994 to 1996, Scott was the deputy regional security officer at the U.S. Embassy in Guatemala City. While in Guatemala he had the opportunity to offer security assistance, advice and briefings to a number of missionaries, missionary organizations, Christian schools and American expatriates.

Prior to joining Stratfor, Scott spent six years with Dell Computer Corporation, where he served as the intelligence coordinator for Dell's Global Security Division and as a leader on Michael Dell's executive protective team.

Scott's experiences as a committed Christian and loving husband and father, and his decades of service in a variety of church leadership roles, have helped provide him with the background to address security topics from a Christian perspective. He and his wife also lead a group from their church on an annual short-term mission trip.

Scott frequently lectures on terrorism and security to law enforcement, university and civic groups. He is regularly featured as a security expert in leading media outlets, including The New York Times, the Los Angeles Times, CNN International, NPR, Reuters, USA Today, The Associated Press, World Magazine, Fox News, Discovery Channel and Time magazine.

21393530R00073